WHAT PEOPLE ARE ~~SAYING ABOUT~~ BOB AND CHERYL
MOELLER AND ~~THE 6 HEARTS OF INTIMACY~~

For many couples, sexual ~~intimacy is a source of frustr~~ation. Drawing
heavily from Scriptural in~~sight, the Moellers remind us~~ that 'it's all about
the heart'. For those who want deeper sexual intimacy, the six "heart attitudes" point the way to mutual sexual fulfillment.

—*Gary D. Chapman, Ph.D.*
Author, *The Five Love Languages*

God has blessed Bob and Cheryl Moeller with a very special gift in marriage ministry that is not only saving many marriages, but helping thousands of other couples build stronger marriages. Bob's live call-in show,
Marriage for Better or Worse, was one of TLN's most popular programs.
I was always impressed with Bob's calm demeanor and remarkable spiritual insights, even with the toughest of marriage questions from callers
with marriage problems hard to imagine. But on a more personal level, my
wife and I have a close friend whose marriage was saved through Bob and
Cheryl's marriage ministry. I have no doubt that *The 6 Hearts of Intimacy*,
with its biblical foundation, will have a dramatic positive impact on thousands more marriages. I highly recommend it.

—*Jerry Rose*
Chairman of the Board, Total Living Network

The more I read *The 6 Hearts of Intimacy*, the more I wanted to read.
Authentic. Biblical. Loaded with really great stories, quotes, and illustra-
tions, too! Sex without intimacy—no married couple deliberately chooses
that path. But it's exactly where many end up. Those couples and every
other couple need to read this book.

—*Jon Gauger*
Host, Moody Radio; Author, *If I Could Do It All Over Again*

Bob and Cheryl truly care about the quality of relationships. *The 6 Hearts of Intimacy* is a great tool not only for married couples but also "Marriage 101" for dating and singles. I highly recommend *The 6 Hearts of Intimacy* because it will help people build and nurture lasting, meaningful, godly relationships. I am buying a copy of this book for every couple on my gift list.

—*Leanne Woods*
Community and Church Engagement Director
Safe Families for Children

God designed us to enjoy sexual intimacy but many never experience it. Bob and Cheryl present the loving, biblical guidelines the Designer intended. *The 6 Hearts of Intimacy* will energize any marriage!

—*Chris Fabry*
Author, *Dogwood, June Bug*, and *War Room: Prayer Is a Powerful Weapon*

I didn't think I could love my husband deeper or appreciate him more. But after reading *The 6 Hearts of Intimacy*, I do just that. This is the best book on marital intimacy I have ever read!

—*Marcia Robertson Lauber*
Retired Clinical and High School Counselor, Plymouth High School, IN

You've learned about sex in school, from friends, in the streets, your own relationships, and maybe your own home. You're convinced there's nothing more to learn. Your marriage suffers because of it, yet you don't believe this. Sexuality is a gift from God, given to us to strengthen our marriage relationship. It's time to learn about sex from its Creator. Start with *The 6 Hearts of Intimacy*.

—*Shando Valdez*
Senior Pastor, New Jerusalem Baptist Church, Chicago, IL

Amazing writing. Since "everything flows from the heart," great lovers must certainly have healthy hearts. Bob and Cheryl have done a masterful job at mining the Scriptures and sharing stories that will heal your heart and open the floodgates of love. Read *The 6 Hearts of Intimacy* and get ready to love like never before.

—*Karl Clauson*
Radio Host, *Karl & Crew*, Moody Radio; Lead Pastor, 180 Chicago

The 6 Hearts of Intimacy will awaken and mature the heart of your marriage. Learn God's wisdom for your marriage and break out of your rut to discover the marriage you first dreamed about.

—*Ron Deal*
Speaker, Therapist, and Author, *The Smart Stepfamily* and
The Smart Stepfamily Marriage

The

6

Hearts of

INTIMACY

ENJOY DEEPER LOVE AND
PASSION IN MARRIAGE

BOB & CHERYL MOELLER

WHITAKER
HOUSE

THE 6 HEARTS OF INTIMACY
Enjoy Deeper Love and Passion in Marriage

For Better For Worse For Keeps Ministries
www.forkeepsministries.com
info@forkeepsministries.com

ISBN: 978-1-64123-160-2
eBook ISBN: 978-1-62911-996-0
Printed in the United States of America
© 2018 by Bob and Cheryl Moeller

Whitaker House
1030 Hunt Valley Circle
New Kensington, PA 15068
www.whitakerhouse.com

Library of Congress Cataloging-in-Publication Data
Names: Moeller, Bob, author. | Moeller, Cheryl, author.
Title: The six hearts of intimacy : enjoy deeper love and passion in marriage
    / Bob and Cheryl Moeller.
Description: New Kensington, PA : Whitaker House, [2018] | Includes
    bibliographical references.
Identifiers: LCCN 2018017413 | ISBN 9781641231602 (alk. paper)
Subjects: LCSH: Marriage—Religious aspects—Christianity. | Intimacy
    (Psychology)—Religious aspects—Christianity.
Classification: LCC BV835 .M6435 2018 | DDC 248.8/44—dc23 LC record available at
https://lccn.loc.gov/2018017413

1 2 3 4 5 6 7 8 9 10 11 WH 25 24 23 22 21 20 19 18

CONTENTS

1

HEARTS TO HEARTS

Bob's father escaped the clutches of death to wind up in his mother's arms.

Homer Moeller was in flight training at age twenty when the world was at war. It was a sunny, blazing hot morning in Tucson, Arizona, when he and nine other brave men swung into the underbelly of a large airplane and began going through a pre-flight checklist.

When all was ready for take-off, Homer pushed the throttles forward and gunned the four giant propeller engines. A deafening roar shook the plane down to the last rivet as they slowly began to rumble down the runway, headed for the wild blue yonder.

Then something went wrong—terribly wrong.

As Homer pulled back on the rounded yoke of the plane to point heavenward, the plane stubbornly refused to lift off. Not until he and the other pilot almost pulled the steering yokes from the floor were they able to get the plane off the ground. They were only a few hundred feet from the end of the runway and certain catastrophe.

Instead of soaring into the air, the plane fought them at every turn when they tried to gain altitude. Something strange and unexpected was happening. Each time Homer pushed the wing flaps' controls forward to make the plane go up, it went down instead. When he reversed the flaps, the plane would climb higher—the opposite of everything a plane is supposed to do.

Knowing disaster was imminent, Homer made a split-second decision. Finally gaining a little altitude, he took the plane into a sharp, 180-degree turn and headed right back toward the center of the runway from which he had just taken off only minutes earlier.

What saved Homer Moeller's life—and the lives of the other nine men on board—was his decision to change course now, when things were headed on the wrong direction, doing the opposite of what he always did. As he approached the runway for an emergency landing, he set the flaps for take-off instead of a landing—and sure enough, the plane instantly obeyed and allowed him to descend safely onto the runway.

Homer would always grin and shake his head as he later learned what went wrong: "Turns out, the flight line mechanics accidentally attached the wing flap wires on backwards."

We wonder how many married couples feel like their marriage has the wing flap wires on backwards. Nowhere could this be truer than in your life of married sexual intimacy. Try as you might, things just aren't working right. You've been headed in the wrong direction and you know it. What is supposed to bring both of you a sense of loving and being loved is instead producing disappointment, emptiness, and despair. If you are honest, you might even say things are spiraling out of control and threaten to end in a crash-and-burn.

If that's where you are, we pray this book can help.

It's not a book about trying new techniques or positions. It's not about using special herbal supplements or libido boosting diets. It's not about finding exotic getaways or visiting a Lover's Lane store. Such quick fixes are attempts to change the fruit of the problem rather than solve the root of the problem.

The heart is the heart of your life of
sexual love and intimacy.

That's because the heart is the heart of your life of sexual love and intimacy.

When it comes to married sexual love, we believe our Heavenly Father has created Six Hearts of Intimacy. Each is distinct from the other. Each is vital to the way we may give and receive love, and each is taught in Scripture.

Once we understand that our spouse may have a different Heart or Hearts than we do, we can understand why what pleases us may not please them. Once we see that our Creator may have designed people to experience sexual love in different ways, it will help us see what our mate needs from us is different from what we need from them. One Heart is not better or superior to another—it's just different and unique by design. And the way we give and receive love can manifest itself in other aspects of our lives as well.

This book also explains the common counterfeit hearts of intimacy that inevitably produce hurt, frustration, and even anger once they enter into our marriage. We have seen such strong, negative emotions in the faces of people we've worked with. Like the husband who became visibly angry when discussing how his wife had denied his sexual needs for years. Or the wife who broke down and cried as she described the devaluation she experiences from her husband's involvement in pornography.

While sin may be at the root of sexual problems in marriage, a lack of understanding and unhealed hurts from the past can also lead to discord and friction. We may not truly know what our spouse is longing for and how to provide it for them. Nor may we know why past pain locks their heart when it comes to the present joys of sex.

For example, one spouse might long for quick, positive responses to sexual overtures, while the other dreams of texted love notes, a date night each week for just the two of them, or long, sweet moments cuddling on the couch.

Perhaps one yearns to spend a day together listening to some favorite music while working side by side in the yard, then going to dinner at their favorite barbeque place, and ending the evening behind closed doors, enjoying the real dessert. At the same time, the spouse might want the two of them to read the Bible together, pray for their children, and share what they are learning in their walk with God.

Maybe you dream of the day your spouse enters into the act of sexual intimacy with the same sense of ecstasy and elation you experience. At the same time, maybe what your mate really wants is for you to tell your friends and family he or she "is everything I ever wanted—my one and only."

Why is it you just can't seem to get on the same page?

Are Your Hearts in Sync—or Sinking?

Let's look at some painful scenarios that occur in many marriages. Not only does one spouse fail to see what the other is seeking in order to find fulfillment and joy in their sexual relationship, they do the very opposite and wound the other's heart in the process.

- Instead of enthusiastically responding to your spouse's request for sex, you act obligated and irritated. Whenever you sense they are feeling amorous, you are conveniently busy, or turn away and go to sleep.

- Rather than responding to your spouse's desire for more romantic moments, you act like that would be tedious. When you are alone at work, you find yourself drawn to the lure of pornography on the Internet, which your spouse eventually discovers.

- Instead of recognizing your spouse's desire for companionship and spending time doing things they enjoy, you say you're too busy with work, chores, or the kids. If your spouse persists, you criticize them and say, "Grow up!"

- Perhaps you consistently turn down your spouse's request to pray or have devotions together. You may even tell them to quit trying to push religion on you. And when the two of you are sharing physical intimacy, you pressure them to do things they find uncomfortable or even degrading. When you're told "no, I don't want to," you say, "You're such a wuss. I wish I had married someone who enjoyed experimenting and having fun."

+ When your spouse asks if you are enjoying the sexual experience as much as they are, you send the message you are bored and just want to get it over with, or find it disgusting.

+ Your spouse asks you not to have lunch with coworker of the opposite sex and you accuse them of being too sensitive, immature, or jealous. Others might be tempted by time alone with members of the opposite sex, but *you* can handle it. After work, you meet some coworkers—without your spouse—for drinks and socializing, for an hour or two. Or three...

All of these scenarios have something in common.

It's a heart problem. In some cases, a serious heart problem. Each person has failed to understand the Six Hearts of Intimacy that God designed for us to give and receive love. Instead, each has become self-focused on their own needs and failed to understand the heart of the spouse.

All of our hearts are alike in their need to love and be loved, to cherish and be cherished, and to care and be cared for. Yet how we express that love—particularly in area of sexual intimacy in marriage—often differs greatly. What brings satisfaction to you may be optional for your wife or husband. What you truly long for in sexual intimacy may not be at all what your spouse is praying you'll provide.

When we fail to understand our spouse's heart, we inevitably end up failing to provide for their legitimate, created, and God-given needs. Like the pizza driver who shows up three hours late, we simply fail to deliver.

The Six Hearts of Intimacy

Which brings us to what we believe is the solution. From our study of Scripture, we have come to identify Six Hearts of Intimacy. Each of these hearts are taken from passages in the Bible devoted to discussing married sexual love.

They are:

+ The Romantic Heart
+ The Worshipping Heart
+ The Companion Heart
+ The Giving Heart
+ The Ecstatic Heart
+ The Guardian Heart

In the coming chapters, we will go into greater detail regarding the nature of these hearts. Based on Scripture, we will examine the unique characteristics of each, how each heart has its counterfeit in our world today and, finally, how we can care for each of the Six Hearts and how to apply them to our marriage.

Our prayer is that there will be a new beginning in your life of married sexual love. We hope any frustration, discord, or hidden anger you've experienced will become a thing of the past.

We pray your spouse will understand how you feel loved, wanted, and admired when they truly enjoy providing for your physical needs; how joyful and gratified you feel when you both enjoy the intoxicating thrill of the sexual act; and how your heart is filled with gladness when you view each other as soul-mates, emotional comrades, and loyal companions in life.

We pray your spouse will learn to provide you with an emotionally intimate, thoughtful, and imaginative atmosphere; take the initiative in leading you into an awareness of Christ's Presence and blessing even in your act of physical consummation; and, finally, give you deep, emotional security and assurance by affirming both by words and behaviors their commitment to an exclusive, life-long covenant of faithfulness.

As you discover the heart is the heart of all relationships, including your sexual relationship, we hope you will discover the causes of any struggles you've had. More importantly, we hope you will discover real and practical solutions in achieving the lasting fulfillment and intimacy you both desire.

It may begin by discovering—just as Homer did at the controls of his plane on that fateful day—that if something isn't working, it's time to do something different before it's too late.

A Coded Heart for Romance

His service during World War II gave Homer some interesting ideas about romance.

While he was completing his military training in Texas, his sweetheart, Inez, was living with her folks on a farm in the Midwest. Separated by more than one thousand miles and seeking privacy away from the prying eyes of his buddies, Homer rented a small rowboat and paddled out to the middle of a lake. There, he scribbled a brief note to Inez and tucked it inside a small black box holding a diamond ring.

Of course, she was excited to unwrap his package and find the sparkling ring. But Homer's note wasn't easy to decipher. Written in dots and dashes, it read:

.-- .. .-.. .-..   -.-- --- ..-   -- .- .-. .-. -.-- -- . ..--..

Inez had her suspicions about what the note meant, but she drove into town anyway to visit the library and translate his message in Morse Code:

"Will you marry me?"

Homer Moeller's proposal exhibited his version of the Romantic Heart. It must have worked—they were married for fifty-five years.

Questions to Consider:

1. Why are we often so reluctant to change course in our relationships even when things aren't working?

2. Why is it important to understand the things that can damage our hearts and prevent us from giving and receiving love?

3. Is it possible that cultivating the Six Hearts of Intimacy could significantly improve a couple's life of sexual intimacy?

God's Word to Consider:

*"Then God said, 'Let us make men in our image, in our likeness...
So God created man in his own image, in the image of God he created
him; male and female he created them.'"*   (Genesis 1:26–27)

2

THE ROMANTIC HEART

*Let my lover come into his garden and taste its choice fruits. I have
come into my garden, my sister, my bride: I have gathered my myrrh
and my spice....I have eaten my honeycomb and my honey;
I have drunk my wine and my milk.*
—Song of Songs 4:16, 5:1

Romance—a feeling of excitement and mystery associated with
love...Love, especially when sentimental or idealized...A quality or
feeling of mystery, excitement and remoteness from everyday life.[1]

The Romantic Heart gives and receives love by bonding with our eyes,
stirring our spouse's emotional imagination with our words, and creating intimacy with our time alone together.

*If you create the right atmosphere for sex,
then you create the desire for sex.*

---

1. https://en.oxforddictionaries.com/definition/romance

How Bob Met Cheryl

Bob says, "I was love sick and there wasn't a thing I could do about it. Nor did I want to.

"When I saw Cheryl for the first time, she was twenty-one years old and I was twenty-three. I was immediately smitten. What you might call emotional roadkill. Although the bookstore hallway at our seminary was brimming with students jostling textbooks, class schedules, and last-minute school supplies, amidst all of the voices and frenzy, time suddenly stood still. For there, I first gazed upon this beautiful woman dressed in a fashionable green jacket and skirt.

"Who was she? What was her name? Where was she from?

"All of those questions swirled in my mind like an Oklahoma prairie twister in April. As suddenly as she had appeared, she quickly disappeared into the crowd of students scurrying to arrive at class on time. While she may have vanished from my sight, she lingered on in my mind and now racing heart.

"From friends, I soon learned her name was Cheryl. She was a first-year student in the Master of Religious Education program. She was from Michigan. In the days to come, I would seek whatever more information I could gain about this beautiful woman who had arrived so unexpectedly on campus. I would scan the cafeteria, walk through the library, and search the hallways just to catch another glimpse of this blonde-haired beauty who had captured my imagination.

"A person that attractive does not go unnoticed for long. Soon, would-be suitors were all around her. To my stunning disappointment, I soon learned she was now dating a fellow classmate. Did that mean I should I give up on pursuing her? Had I been too slow to introduce myself? After all, what were the chances this lucky guy wouldn't cling to her like a cat dangling from the top of the living room curtains?

"Despite my apparently day-late-and-dollar-short status, something inside me said, 'Don't give up.' As warm September turned to colorful October then to chilly November, I heard some startling news one day. She and the Other Guy were going to break up at 5:30 p.m. that Friday.

"My heart leapt with joy as I knew this was my second chance. Lovers and parachute jumpers have one thing in common: As the earth starts getting closer and closer, you'd better pull the ripcord now, or you'll end up dead on arrival.

"What was going on in Cheryl's mind about me during this long fall season of unrequited love I was caught up in? Apparently not much.

"She claims the first time she took notice of me was several weeks after school started when I was standing on top of a cafeteria table doing my Billy Graham impersonation. Those who know me today as the quiet, shy, and somewhat introverted guy who turns red when his number is called over the speaker at the Motor Vehicle Department may have trouble believing this story. But if it meant pretending I was a world renowned evangelist preaching to multitudes at the Los Angeles Coliseum just to get a pretty girl's attention—well, I was all in. Men will do strange things when they are in love."

What Cheryl Remembers

I walked into our school cafeteria one day for the obligatory salad plate, bowl of minestrone soup, and green Jell-O dessert when I noticed a six-foot guy with a Bible flopping in one hand and his other hand pointing upward. He was speaking in a voice that sounded remarkably like Billy Graham. He thundered from atop the cafeteria table as if preaching to thousands.

He then had his good friend climb up next to him and lead the cafeteria in a hymn just like the famous song leader Cliff Barrows would in stadiums where Billy Graham preached.

He wasn't actually giving an altar call. Instead, he was inviting other students to sign up to work at a Christian music festival he was chairman of that year. At first, I thought this guy is a little crazy, then I thought, no, he's actually funny. While it might not have been love at first sight, he definitely had my attention.

Bob started showing up at my table at lunch and sitting down. He asked me if I'd be interested in volunteering for the music festival. He gave me coveted jobs I didn't deserve, like working directly with big national singing groups. I thought he was just looking for volunteers, like some United Way recruiter. What he was really after (I found out later) was a Way for us to be United in marriage.

In the weeks to come, I discovered this guy was fun to be with. It didn't hurt that he was smart, six feet tall, and had brown hair, hazel green eyes, perfect teeth, and a Minnesota Nice personality. Bob told me he won the state championship in debate in high school and I soon learned he definitely had a way with words. It didn't matter where I was—in the library, in chapel, or just walking across campus, Mr. Minnesota Nice always seemed to show up.

I started to find myself attracted to him. I returned his smiles. I lingered longer in conversations. He drove a big car his Dad had given him, so I thought he might be loaded. Turns out the only thing loaded about him were the baked potatoes he ordered with extra butter, bacon, and cheddar cheese. But he was also rich in his appetite for God. My heart started to beat a little faster when the phone rang and his voice was on the line. After our first date, I knew I was falling in love.

With the Other Guy Out of the Way...

After the break-up with the Other Guy, we went out. That was followed by more time spent together. We would walk to class, study together in the library, and sometimes eat supper across the table from one another.

The times we valued the most, however, were the times when it was just the two of us—what we call being "alone together." We would stand outside on many balmy Kentucky evenings in late fall—talking, laughing, and looking into one another's eyes. It was as if some giant tractor beam from *Star Trek* had locked on to our hearts and was pulling us ever closer into each other's orbits.

Our Romantic Hearts were beating—a hundred times a minute or more.

Bob says, "It was as if some giant love lever within my heart had been pushed into full throttle position. My romantic love gears were spinning so fast, Cheryl was all I could think of day and night. During Christmas break, I went home to Minnesota and had four wisdom teeth pulled out. Though my mouth now had four miniature empty pits to rinse out each day, my heart was filled to the brim with joy.

"When I returned to campus in January, Cheryl had left for the month to perform in Florida with a touring drama group from campus. Missing her terribly, I made the near fatal mistake of taking ancient Hebrew as a class that month. I was supposed to be memorizing vocabulary words from the book of Deuteronomy; unfortunately, the only ones I could remember were those starting with 'ch.' I stared at a photo of Cheryl and kept thinking about things she had said or written to me, trying to detect clues that she felt as strongly about me as I did about her. The result? I got the first big fat 'C' of my entire academic career that month. It was fine. After all, 'C' was the first letter of Cheryl's name.

"My feelings for Cheryl only got stronger with time. I was love sick. I dropped to 149 pounds. Who needed food? More than one evening, I walked into the cafeteria, glanced at the steaming steel tables of food, and walked out. I'd wander back to my dormitory room and write Cheryl yet another love note.

"As the magnolia trees began to blossom in Kentucky that spring, so did my Romantic Heart and the conviction I had met my future wife. I started to keep a journal describing my deep feelings of love for her, something I'd never done before. I began writing poetry for her and gave it to her to read. When romantic songs came on the radio, I sang along. If romance is an illness, I definitely belonged in the Intensive Care Unit at this point.

"It all culminated in one glorious moment the night I got down on my knees and asked Cheryl to marry me. I loved how her eyes glistened as she nodded yes. In a matter of a few minutes, we were on the phone calling everyone we knew (and even a few wrong numbers) to announce we were engaged."

Love Makes You Do Crazy Things

Being crazy in love is not unusual. It happens all of the time. And it can seriously alter the behavior of otherwise rational, emotionally stable men and women. Consider just a couple unusual proposals we gleaned from the Internet:

- ❖ The Thrilled to Death Proposal: A young man faked his own death in front of his girlfriend. While she wept uncontrollably over his lifeless corpse, he suddenly sat up, opened his eyes, and popped the question. (It's not known whether she popped him one in the face.)

- ❖ The Download Proposal 3.0. Some ingenious young man managed to persuade Groupon, the discount coupon website, to feature a coupon entitled, "The Deal of a Lifetime—Me." When he directed his young lady to the website, she was amazed that true love was just a click away. Apparently, she added him permanently to her shopping cart. (We don't know if Amazon Prime delivered him to her door with free shipping.)

The Romantic Heart Defined

What did these two love-struck males have in common besides the possible need for medication? Each had discovered the Romantic Heart, the first of the Six Hearts of Intimacy.

Why is the longing for romance such a powerful, life-long driving force? Because God created it to be this way. Just as all of the Six Hearts of Intimacy find their origin in the heart of God so does the Romantic Heart. This truth is seen throughout Scripture.

It occurs when Adam first sees Eve and is overcome by her beauty and perfection. After being introduced to Eve by God Himself, he declares, "*This is now bone of my bones and flesh of my flesh*" (Genesis 2:23). The Romantic Heart finds its most lengthy and eloquent expression in the Song of Songs, wherein the bride exclaims, "*I am weak with love*" (Song of Songs 2:5). It is expressed in narrative form in the amazing love story of God wooing the heart of Israel in the Book of Ezekiel.

It doesn't end with the Old Testament either. In the New Testament, the Romantic Heart continues on in full display as Jesus performs his first miracle at the wedding feast in Cana of Galilee. Paul expresses the spiritual mystery of the Romantic Heart as he draws the parallel of a couple's love for each other to Christ's deep affection for His church. The Bible ends with the glorious celebration of the Wedding Supper of the Lamb in the Book of Revelation. All throughout the Bible, the Romantic Heart is celebrated as a reflection of the Heart of our Triune God.

Let's take one example of God's Romantic Heart found in Ezekiel. God likens His heart-felt love for Israel to a man who happens upon a field and finds a female infant abandoned by her parents. She is certain to die if someone does not care for her. God's heart is moved by her perilous condition and He rescues her.

Through the years, He tenderly cares for her and nurtures the child, all the while jealously guarding her modesty and virtue. Then when she reaches adulthood, He pursues her heart for marriage. Ultimately, they are joined in holy matrimony. Like an ecstatic husband in love with His bride, He lavishes her with expensive gifts, elegant clothing, and glittering jewels fit for a queen. Listen to the Romantic Heart of God express His love for His beloved bride Israel:

> I gave you my solemn oath and entered into a covenant with you, declares the Sovereign LORD, and you became mine... I clothed you with an embroidered dress and put sandals of fine leather on you. I dressed you in fine linen and covered you with costly garments. I adorned you with jewelry: I put bracelets on your arms and a necklace around your neck, and I put a ring on your nose, earrings on your ears and a beautiful crown on your head. So you were adorned with gold and silver; your clothes were of fine linen and costly fabric and embroidered cloth. Your food was honey, olive oil and the finest flour. You became very beautiful and rose to be a queen. And your fame spread among the nations on account of your beauty, because the splendor I had given you made your beauty perfect, declares the Sovereign LORD. (Ezekiel 16:4–14)

Romance is God's gift to couples to bring exquisite and lifelong joy to their relationship.

Clearly, God is using the analogy of a man falling rapturously in love with a woman and treating her as a royal queen. Romance is neither carnal nor silly—it is a gift from a holy, loving God given to couples to bring exquisite and lifelong joy to their relationship.

The Basic Elements of the Romantic Heart

Let's look at each of these three basic elements of the Romantic Heart and how they impact our sexual relationship in marriage.

The legendary detective Sherlock Holmes was famous for his uncanny ability to discover a simple solution to what often appeared to be an unsolvable mystery. He found clues that others overlooked. For instance, in the story *Silver Blaze*, Holmes cites "the curious incident of the dog in the night-time" as a pivotal clue. Since it did not bark, the dog knew the person who took the race horse very well.

Fortunately, we don't have to be expert sleuths when it comes to understanding the workings of the Romantic Heart. Here are three important characteristics:

1. Using your eyes to create a visual bond with one another

2. Using your *words* to stir imagination and excitement

3. Using your time alone to create a special sense of closeness

We find each of these three elements of the Romantic Heart in the Bible's most celebrated book of married sexual love—the Song of Songs, sometimes called the Song of Solomon.

Let's briefly look at each of these three vital components of the Romantic Heart.

1. Using your eyes to visually bond with the one you love.

In the early chapters of the Song of Songs, we hear the blushing new bride of Solomon describing how her husband uses his eyes to arouse deep feelings of romance. *"My lover is like a young gazelle or a young stag. Look! There he stands behind our wall, peering through the lattice"* (Song of Songs 2:9).

One of the early steps in the romantic bonding process between a man and woman is eye-to-eye contact. This bride catches Solomon gazing at her through the lattice and their eyes meet. His fixed stare causes her heart to leap. She finds his eyes are connecting to her eyes and creating feelings of intrigue, enjoyment, and emotional arousal.

So powerful is the visual bonding process that the Bible warns us to have eyes for our spouse only. *"For this command is a lamp, this teaching is a light and correction, and instruction are the way to life, keeping you from your neighbor's wife....Do not lust in your heart after her beauty or let her captivate you with her eyes"* (Proverbs 6:23–25).

Your future spouse may have been surprised, perhaps even slightly embarrassed, the first time you found yourselves staring at each other. But perhaps each of you felt complimented by the fact that someone was looking at you in a decidedly different way. Years later, we still enjoy having our husband or wife gazing at us for long periods of time. Their eyes tell us we are special to them.

Isn't it true that when people fall deeply in love, they find it hard to look at anyone else? Connecting eye to eye is vital to creating intimacy during the sexual act. Of all the creatures God created on this beautiful earth, only human beings were made to face each other so they could look into one another's eyes during the act of physical intimacy. One writer compared this eye-to-eye intimacy to touching an electric socket. The electricity and energy it generates is overpowering and magnificent.

However, those who only have that "look in their eye" when they desire sex are going to shortchange their spouses' desire for the Romantic Heart. People like to have their spouses notice them, admire them, and give them their attention all day long, not just when their spouses are in the mood for sex. We want them to want to know our hearts, not just our bodies.

An Open Window to the Soul

If you want to truly care for your spouse's Romantic Heart, make sustained eye contact each day. You will soon discover the truth of what Jesus said, *"The light of the body is the eye"* (Matthew 6:22). Your eyes are a special romantic pathway that leads directly to your spouse's heart.

When you were dating, maybe you whispered to your sweetheart, "I just can't take my eyes off of you" or "I love how your eyes sparkle and are so playful." Those are words your beloved always wants to hear.

Most people want their spouses to notice them. That's why, when we are in love, we spend so much time on our appearance—hair, make-up, necktie, shirt or blouse, pants or skirt, jewelry, sport coat, handbag, belt, socks, nail polish, and just the right shoes. We want to feel beautiful or handsome. This desire does not evaporate the moment we say "I do," or step off the airplane back home after the honeymoon. Our spouses appreciate it when we dress to please them.

Bob says, "I'll never forget standing at the door of Cheryl's dormitory in the spring moonlight and just gazing into her big, beautiful brown eyes. The longer I looked into those eyes, the more she smiled—a smile that came directly from her Romantic Heart."

Talking Directly to the Heart

God has designed the Romantic Heart so that when we visually connect for long periods of time, our hearts begin to emotionally bond with one another.

One exercise we use to help couples struggling in their marriages to regain a sense of emotional intimacy is to have them turn their chairs toward one another and hold hands. We ask them look into each other's eyes and nowhere else. Then we coach them to speak words of tenderness and love to each other such as, "I think your heart just wants me to cherish you and treat you as my one and only in life. Would you mind if I did that?" Or, "Your heart is so precious to me, I feel like I'm the luckiest person on earth. Is it okay to feel that way?" We have witnessed many people's eyes well up with tears as they nod their heads.

For many couples, this is the first time they have experienced emotional intimacy in months—or even years. Suddenly, they realize their hearts are connecting and they get excited.

There are times we should let our eyes do all the talking.

Imagine what will happen when you spend sustained time looking into each other's eyes during the act of sexual intimacy. Try it and find out. Visual focus has a way of filling the Romantic Heart to the brim and then some. There are times we should let our eyes do all the talking. Sex may be one of those rare opportunities to do just that.

2. Use your words to stir imagination and excitement.

We often remind couples at our marriage conferences that words are little pathways to a person's soul. They are among the most priceless elements of the Romantic Heart. It is not only what we say but how we say it that stirs our beloved's romantic imagination. If looking into your spouse's eyes is the first passageway to the Romantic Heart, then using words to stir imagination and mystery is the second.

What if you don't feel you're good with words? No problem. Use what other people have written. You can find many expressions of romantic, passionate love in popular music from almost any genre. Or try reading brief excerpts from romantic literary classics to stir your spouse's heart and imagination.

Start with this passage from Jane Austen's tale of a tempestuous and complicated romance set in eighteenth century England, simply entitled, *Persuasion*. Here, a young man proposes a second time to the woman who rebuffed his first offer of marriage years earlier:

> "You pierce my soul. I am half agony, half hope. Tell me not that I am too late, that such precious feelings are gone forever. I offer myself to you again with a heart even more your own than when you almost broke it, eight years and a half ago. Dare not say that man forgets sooner than woman, that his love has an earlier death. I have loved none but you."[2]

Or how about this stirring proclamation from William Goldman's *The Princess Bride*:

> "I thought an hour ago that I loved you more than any woman has ever loved a man, but a half hour after that I knew that what I felt

2. Jane Austen, *Persuasion* (Oxford, England: Oxford University Press, 2004)

before was nothing compared to what I felt then. But ten minutes after that, I understood that my previous love was a puddle compared to the high seas before a storm."[3]

Or this tortured confession of love taken from *Our Mutual Friend* by Charles Dickens:

"You know what I am going to say. I love you. What other men may mean when they use that expression, I cannot tell; what I mean is, that I am under the influence of some tremendous attraction which I have resisted in vain and which overmasters me...This and the confusion of my thoughts, so that I am fit for nothing, is what I mean by your being the ruin of me..."[4]

Preventing a Romantic Dust Bowl

When we fail to use words to stir a sense of imagination and mystery, particularly for our spouse's Romantic Heart, it can create an emotional drought in their life. It leaves them parched and thirsting to hear our expressions of love. It feels like living in the salt flats of Death Valley day after day.

Husbands and wives experience romantic drought when they go for weeks, months, or even years without hearing words of imagination and mystery from us. Their Romantic Heart eventually feels barren and forsaken. Once people conclude their spouses have lost interest in romance, they may in turn lose their interest and enthusiasm for sexual overtures.

Your Love Life Ignited by Fresh Produce?

If you're still at a loss for just the right romantic words, perhaps wise King Solomon can come to the rescue. Romantic words that stir mystery and imagination are interspersed throughout the Song of Songs. While the word pictures Solomon uses to flatter his new bride may seem a little odd or even insulting (like comparing his beloved's hair to a flock of goats), it's only because we don't take the time to translate them into modern parlance.

---

3. William Goldman, *The Princess Bride* (Boston: Houghton Mifflin Harcourt, 2007)
4. *Our Mutual Friend* available at: https://www.gutenberg.org/files/883/883-h/883-h.htm

When it comes to using just the right words to stir a woman's Romantic Heart, Solomon knew what he was doing. According to the Scriptures, he was the wisest man of his generation.

> *God gave Solomon wisdom and very great insight, and a breadth of understanding as measureless as the sand on the seashore. Solomon's wisdom was greater than the wisdom of all the people of the East, and greater than all the wisdom of Egypt. He was wiser than anyone else.*
>
> (1 Kings 4:29–31)

We'll first give you his version of how to stir a woman's heart with words and then translate them into modern language:

> *How beautiful you are, my darling! Oh, how beautiful! Your eyes behind your veil are doves. Your hair is like a flock of goats descending from the hills of Gilead.*
>
> *Your teeth are like a flock of sheep just shorn, coming up from the washing. Each has its twin; not one of them is alone.*
>
> *Your lips are like a scarlet ribbon; your mouth is lovely. Your temples behind your veil are like the halves of a pomegranate.*
>
> *Your neck is like the tower of David, built with courses of stone; on it hang a thousand shields, all of them shields of warriors.*
>
> *Your breasts are like two fawns, like twin fawns of a gazelle that browse among the lilies. Until the day breaks and the shadows flee, I will go to the mountain of myrrh and to the hill of incense.*
>
> *You are altogether beautiful, my darling; there is no flaw in you.*
>
> (Song of Songs 4:1–7)

At a Christian men's conference, popular author/lecturer John Eldredge observed that in this passage, Solomon starts at the top of his wife's body and works his way down. As he read it aloud, the husbands in the audience spontaneously broke out into applause and loud cheers.

Was cheering for the physical features of a wife that a husband finds alluring and exhilarating inappropriate for a Christian men's gathering? At first blush, the answer might be yes—but let's remember they were hearing the Word of God, read word for word.

We should be thankful that the wisest man of his time left us an entire book to explain how to talk to our beloved in a way that leads to high-octane, romantic, married sexual love. It's our guess that if Solomon were alive today, he would be in much demand as a speaker for weekend men's retreats. The dude knew how to stir his wife's imagination.

Okay, let's try translating this passage into modern terms. Our paraphrase goes like this: "Everything about you is as beautiful, majestic, perfectly formed and alluring as anything on earth. Your penetrating eyes beguile me, your smile leaves me weak, your lips set my heart on fire, your face is perfection itself and the idea of caressing you is drowning me in a river of desire for you..."

What are some principles we can glean from how Solomon uses romantic word-pictures to arouse his wife's heart and imagination?

- Exaggerate your spouse's beauty (or virility) and appearance.
- Verbally work your way from the most obvious parts of his or her body to the most private, expressing your wonder and appreciation.
- Emphasize the loving details of their appearance, heart, and personality that set your mate apart from everyone else.

Romantic Help Just a Click Away

We live in the age of the Internet, which has its plusses and minuses. But why not use the Web exclusively for good, noble, and holy purposes? How about surfing the Web to find new loving things to say that will stir your spouse's Romantic Heart?

Here are a few romantic things taken from the web you could send in a text message or jot down in a little note that your spouse would love to read any time of the day:

- Last night, I looked up at the stars and matched each one with a reason why I love you. I was doing great until I ran out of stars.
- I sent an angel to watch over you at night. The angel came back a minute later—he said angels don't watch other angels.

+ If you held eleven roses up to a mirror, you'd be looking at twelve of the most beautiful things in the world.

+ If I had to choose between breathing and loving you, I would use my last breath to say, "I love you."

+ God was showing off when He created you.

Thankfully, we don't have to be poets, authors or songwriters to care for our spouse's Romantic Heart. Other people have done the heavy lifting for us. Go ahead and use what's out there on the Internet to whisper to your beloved when you kiss goodbye in the morning. Drop a sentence or two during a ten-minute cell phone call during lunch. Surprise him or her with a romantic phrase when it's just the two of you sitting on the sofa and the kids are in bed. It may not be long until you two are in bed as well.

Bob's Advice for Added Heat

Bob says, "This is a way to say goodbye I came up with all on my own. One morning, I was headed off to work and Cheryl was still seated at the breakfast table finishing her coffee. I came over to say goodbye. She looked up, expecting the usual quick peck on the forehead and the usual, 'I'll see you at 6:00 tonight.' Instead, that morning, I leaned down and gave her a long, luxurious, sloppy kiss. Afterward, she leaned back to catch her breath. I looked into her eyes and said, 'I want you to think about that all day long and maybe tonight as well.'"

Cheryl Turns Up the Heat—Literally

Cheryl says, "Bob elaborately courted me and won my heart. I love to keep courting Bob with an element of surprise. Sometimes, I get tickets for us to attend an outdoor sports show and look through brochures again with him the next day. I surprised him by clearing a shelf in the refrigerator for his favorite snacks. Once, I brought home three perfume samples and asked Bob which one he liked the best. And he loves it when I make a private barbeque outside under the stars with everything cooked on the grill, even dessert. After all, you know what they say about the way to a man's heart. The Romantic Heart heats up for husbands when the grill is turned on. It isn't long before he is as well."

Better Romance Leads to Better Sex

If you consistently focus with your eyes, use imaginative words to stir your mate's heart, and make time to be alone together, it's going to create exactly the right atmosphere for sexual intimacy to take place. Using romantic language and images during the act of sexual intimacy only heightens excitement and response. Tender, imaginative, and intimate words can hasten and propel you both toward sexual climax.

3. Using time alone to create intimacy.

Although we have been married for almost four decades, we continue to learn new <u>things</u> about each other. It never fails to amaze us what settings or circumstances the other finds to be romantic. For instance, here are some of Cheryl's recent ideas for such occasions:

- Going together to an RV show and walking hand in hand to look at all of the newest models, particularly those with diesel engines that get better mileage.

- Watching TV programs together, such as "Alaska: The Last Frontier" on the Discovery Channel or shows on the History Channel. Cheryl loves it when they catch a bear poacher.

- Walking in the woods together for a couple of hours to enjoy nature and get some exercise. (This also brings out the animals in all of us.)

As you've probably noticed, the common element in all of these curious romantic settings is found in one word: "together." We want to do things together, by ourselves. Almost anything will do. We want to be *alone together.*

That's the essence of our third and final element of the Romantic Heart. It's creating a sense of intimacy by being alone together.

Being alone together can happen almost anywhere.

The good news is this: it can happen almost anywhere—in the organic produce aisle at a supermarket, on a bench at a playground, at the mall sharing a chocolate almond gelato, or sitting at a table outside your favorite coffee shop. Any setting will do if it allows the two of you to be lost in time and each other for just a little while. Forget the expensive dinner downtown or state room on a cruise ship. Watching fireflies dance through the air on a warm summer's night can be just as romantic.

The One Time the Bible Says to Be a Stag

The romantic excitement of time spent alone together is expressed by the exuberant bride in Song of Songs. *"Come away, my beloved, and be like a gazelle or like a young stag on the spice-laden mountains"* (Song of Songs 8:14).

Notice her plea is for Solomon to "come away" with her. She wants him all to herself. She urges him to find a remote place high on the mountains where they can be alone together. You know where it will lead.

A day spent alone together will likely lead to an evening of intimacy.

Our advice: don't try to guess which setting your spouse finds to be the most romantic. Instead, just ask and don't argue. Remember, a day spent alone together, where you have each other all to yourselves, will likely lead to an evening of intimacy.

Try These Romantic Suggestions on for Size

We have great respect for the ministry of Family Life led by Dennis and Barbara Rainey. Here are seven suggestions from their magazine[5] for how to be alone together. Remember, being alone together doesn't mean no one else can be in the same area. It just requires that the two of you feel

---

5. http://www.familylife.com/articles/topics/marriage/staying-married/husbands/20-ideas-for-dating-your-wife

you have separated from the everyday routines of life to enjoy a few precious moments to focus on each other. Here are some things the Raineys suggest:

1. Attend a wedding. Sit in the back row and spend the whole time whispering memories from your own wedding.

2. Make a list of ten things your spouse loves to do (or places where he or she loves to go). Do one of those ten things as your weekly date.

3. Relive your honeymoon by scheduling a twenty-four-hour getaway each month and spend it visiting or doing something new.

4. Spend an evening stargazing and talking about dreams you have for the future.

5. Visit places where you grew up, went to school, vacationed as a child, or other places that hold special memories from the time before you met. Learn more about each other's backgrounds.

6. Take a day off of work and do something special.

7. Take a vacation without your kids, without work and without your cell phones or computers.

If romance is ignited by doing simple things that give you time with just each other, where will it all end? Why not try and find out?

Learn to Speak a New Language

In his perennial bestseller, *The 5 Love Languages: The Secret to Love That Lasts*, Dr. Gary Chapman suggests we all have an "emotional love language" with which we communicate and need others to communicate in that language in order for us to feel loved.[6] These include: giving gifts; physical touch; words of affirmation; acts of service; or quality time spent together. Learn your spouse's love language and then daily speak it to him or her. The romantic sparks will soon fly. Each of his Love Languages can be applied to a couple's life of sexual intimacy. Use your imagination and be prepared for some amazing and satisfying results.

---

6. Gary Chapman, *The 5 Love Languages: The Secret to Love That Lasts* (Chicago: Northfield Publishing, 1992)

A Counterfeit of the Romantic Heart

One day, we pulled up to a service station and after we filled our car, we went inside to pay. The smallest bill we had at the time was a $20 bill. The cashier promptly turned around and fed the currency through a machine. It popped out the other side and only then she did she open the cash register and drop it inside.

"What was all that about?" we asked curiously.

"Just checking to see it was for real."

"You get that many fake bills here?"

"More than you'd ever imagine," she answered.

Counterfeits are a real problem in our society. According to the United States Department of Treasury, an estimated $70 million in counterfeit bills are in circulation.[7] Unfortunately, counterfeits exist in married relationships as well.

*The Unfeeling Heart shuts down all of our feelings of
sympathy or compassion.*

The primary counterfeit of the Romantic Heart is the Unfeeling Heart. This heart is characterized by shutting down all of our feelings of sympathy or compassion and living life simply on an intellectual level. We may utter romantic words to our spouses, but we don't feel or mean them. We watch as our mates struggle with damaged emotions or hurts, yet we feel little or no empathy for them. We may go through the motions of romance by buying a card, flowers, or special treat, but our Unfeeling Heart just isn't in it.

As a result, we do just the opposite of the basic elements of the Romantic Heart. We spend little time looking into our spouse's eyes except when we are angry at them. Instead of using words of imagination and mystery, we resort to sarcasm or putdowns to get what we want, when we want it.

---

7. https://en.wikipedia.org/wiki/Counterfeit_United_States_currency

For the Unfeeling Heart, love-making is self-focused, hurried, and lacking any real sense of intimacy. Seldom is any thought given to spending time alone together to nurture the relationship.

The Unfeeling Heart is more common in marriages than you might imagine. It's one reason why the television series *Desperate Housewives* drew such a vast audience. Each episode featured lonely, ignored, and frustrated housewives whose husbands made little or no effort to reach their Romantic Hearts. The hurting and angry women turned to alcohol, prescription drugs, and adultery to counter their romantic deficit.

Post-Honeymoon Flat Line Romance

Fred and Brenda Stoeker in their excellent book entitled, *Every Heart Restored*, share the testimonies of two women who found themselves in marriages characterized by the Unfeeling Heart.[8] While neither marriage could hardly be described as abusive, they both suffered from a serious deficit—their husbands did not display the Romantic Heart:

Jeannine describes how romance ended the day she got married:

"Up until our engagement, Trent treated me with great consideration. We had long conversations and thing I liked most is that we laughed together. As we dated longer and longer, there were many expressions of affection, both verbally and through hugs and kisses. But once Trent put that ring on my finger, it was as if he no longer had to woo me to get what he wanted, so why bother? He started doing whatever he wanted, whether I liked it or not. That attitude pretty well defines our sexual relationship since our wedding."

Then there's Chrissie, who watched their romance replaced by channel surfing:

"I have now been married for almost a year to the only guy I ever dated and I love him very much; he is my brother in Christ and my best friend. But my romantic feelings for him have pretty much

---

8. Fred, and Brenda Stoeker with Mike Yorkey, *Every Heart Restored* (Colorado Springs, Colorado: Waterbrook Press, 2004), pp. 80-81.

flat-lined because he ignores me romantically. I love the intimacy of a hug and extra attention, but the most fulfilling aspects of our relationships have pretty much disappeared. Calling out, 'Hey, you're a babe' when I pass through the room as he channel surfs endlessly hardly measures up to actually taking the time with me after a hard day at work. Yet he seems to expect me to be turned on every time we touch."

If somehow you have allowed the Unfeeling Heart to replace the Romantic Heart in your marriage, you need to ask yourself a simple question: Is this how Jesus wants me to treat my spouse?

The apostle Paul answers this question in no uncertain terms. *"Husbands, love your wives, just as Christ loved the church and gave himself up for her to make her holy, cleansing her by the washing with water through the Word and to present her to himself as a radiant church"* (Ephesians 5:25–27).

Let's just focus for a moment on this one word—radiant. This word should capture, captivate and convict you. When was the last time you touched your beloved's Romantic Heart so deeply that it made him or her smile with radiance?

Bob relates, "I witnessed radiance in Cheryl's eyes the night I proposed to her. I got down on my knees in the living room, looked up, and said, 'Will you marry me?' It took a moment for the full import of my question to reach her heart. But the moment it did, her eyes lit up and a smile broke out with a radiance that almost required sunglasses."

We Are All Romantics at Heart

What child doesn't dream of one day becoming a beautiful princess or a handsome prince or superhero? Until boys start thinking girls are "yucky"—usually when they start school—they are sweetly loving and kind to the little girls they meet. They are royalty, heroes, and heroines in their innocent playtime adventures.

In some cultures, the fairytale idea of becoming a prince or princess never fades. Some good friends of ours showed us pictures of their daughter's wedding day. In their favorite one, she wore an elegant dress as she sat on a chair, posed in regal fashion, and wearing a glittering tiara. Their custom, going back many generations, is for the bride to wear a crown on her wedding day. The radiant smile on her face said it all. For one glorious day, the romantic dream of becoming someone's princess had come true.

Caring for the Romantic Heart

A radio station did a survey of what women wanted most as a gift on Valentine's Day. The answer topping the list was, "I want a date with him that I don't have to plan." Second on the list? "I'd like to sleep as long as I want to."

Notice that the gift they would treasure the most is any romantic experience they didn't have to suggest, hint at or beg for their mates to provide. They weren't asking for a weekend at a spa with Swedish massages, terry cloth bathrobes, facials, and manicures. They weren't asking for a strolling violinist following them down the driveway. They only wanted a date they didn't have to plan.

So here are our two simple suggestions to care for the Romantic Heart:

1. Nurture romance by looking for long periods of time into your spouse's eyes, use imaginative words to stir the imagination and spend generous amounts time alone together.

2. Repeat the above instructions as often as possible.

Your "better half" will never, ever outgrow their need for romance in your marriage. You may live together five years, ten years, or even fifty years, and your spouse will long for you to romance his or her heart.

Don't think for one moment that your spouse doesn't want to be romanced.

Don't think for one moment that your spouse doesn't want to be romanced. Men and women alike want to know you enjoy spending time with them, sharing a laugh with them, being playful, and learning about things that interest them. There are plenty of things you can do together that will bring you closer. Watch sports together. Take a cooking class.

Work on a car. Go shopping. Play a game. Learn a foreign language and plan a vacation to a country where it's spoken. We're sure you can think of dozens of things if you put your hearts and heads together.

If you care for your spouse's Romantic Heart in an unselfish, sacrificial manner, as Christ loves the church, get ready for your love life to go into overdrive. The Romantic Heart is so important that if you nurture and encourage it properly, it will ignite a desire for regular sexual intimacy that may leave you waving a white flag.

If you don't believe us, try it and see.

No Expiration Date

For many, the appeal of the Romantic Heart does not dim with either marriage or age. A dear friend of ours was widowed after enjoying more than fifty years of marriage. She surprised us one day when she called with breathless excitement to tell us she was being pursued by an old acquaintance. He, too, had also recently lost his spouse.

"I'm embarrassed to admit it at my age," she giggled, "but I have strong feelings for him. Do you think that's all right?" The relentless beat of the Romantic Heart was still going strong in her eighth decade of life.

We know a husband whose wife developed Alzheimer's and he took care of her all on his own. Rather than resenting the task, he welcomed the opportunity to show his love during this most difficult season of their marriage. Because of the effects of the disease, she was prone to walking around in their dark home in the middle of the night. She could have easily fallen and hurt herself. Worse yet, she could have wandered outside and gotten lost.

So her adoring husband hit upon an idea to keep her safe from harm. He used a piece of cloth to tie his foot to her foot at night. If she tried to get up in the middle of the night, he would immediately know it.

Though she hardly remembered his name at times, she always recognized the touch of his foot and slept peacefully. Until her final days, he would look into her eyes, talk to her using tender, loving words, and spend countless hours with her, just the two of them. They were alone together for almost seven years before she passed away one day with a peaceful smile on her face.

There is no expiration date for the Romantic Heart as long as we are still married. It was not a dozen roses, a candlelight dinner, or an expensive gift that kept romance alive for almost six decades for this dear couple. In the end, it was just a simple strip of cloth binding them foot to foot and heart to heart.

Tie that strip of cloth today to your spouse's Romantic Heart. You will never regret it.

Questions to Consider:

1. Would God create the feelings of romance if they were silly or unimportant?

_____

_____

_____

_____

_____

2. What role does the Romantic Heart play in attracting a couple to one another?

_____

_____

_____

_____

_____

3. Is the Romantic Heart only for the early phases of a couple's relationship or should it play an important role throughout a marriage?

_____

_____

_____

_____

_____

God's Word to Consider:

> *"You have forsaken your first love...do the things you did at first."*
> (Revelation 2:4–5)

3

THE WORSHIPPING HEART

*But for this reason a man will leave his father and mother and be
united to his wife and become one flesh. This is a profound mystery
but I am talking about Christ and the church.*
—Ephesians 5:31–32

The Worshipping Heart gives and receives love by rejoicing in God's
holy presence in sexual intimacy as a couple offers one another sacrificial love and extraordinary honor.

*If the God who created us is holy,
then you can enjoy His gift of sex as holy.*

One of Bob's roommates from college got married a year or so before
we did. Naturally, when he returned from his honeymoon, his former
roommates were all ears—what was it like to be married? Did sex live up
to his expectations?

He grinned like a Cheshire cat left home alone with the refrigerator
door wide open. While he did not share any intimate details, he did say

it was one of the most satisfying experiences of his life. When his bride glanced over at the guys from across the crowded reception room, she guessed what we were talking about and blushed.

The new husband said something that had such a profound impact on Bob that he decided we should incorporate it into our own marriage one day.

"After we reached the honeymoon suite, the first thing we did was to engage in..."

"Yes...?" He really had our attention.

"The first thing we did was to engage in a prolonged and extended time of prayer. We knelt together by our bed and invited God's presence into our new marriage and our life of sexual intimacy."

Keep in mind, these were all college males in their early twenties, coping with libidos and hormones running at near flood-stage levels. It seemed all but impossible that once you were married and free to have all the sex you wanted, you would deliberately put it off in favor of a prolonged prayer meeting. After all, wasn't this the moment he had been waiting for since seventh grade?

Yet as we would learn—and all Christian newlyweds can learn—pausing to invite the presence of Jesus into the marriage bedroom is anything but foolish. Bob remembers growing up with a portrait in his home that depicted Jesus gently knocking on a large wooden door. It was an insightful artist's interpretation of Revelation 3:20: "*Here I am! I stand at the door and knock. If anyone hears my voice and opens the door, I will come in and eat* [fellowship] *with him and He with me.*"

Many have taken this verse to refer to Jesus knocking at the door of our heart in terms of salvation. Yet read in its proper context, it's about a church of believers who had fallen out of fellowship with Christ. It was not about members of a lost, pagan society realizing their need to repent and believe.

Christ is still knocking at the door of every believer's heart, both male and female, and asking permission to enter every room of our life. Those rooms surely must include the bedroom.

Can You Enjoy Sex If God Is Watching?

The Worshipping Heart knows sexual intimacy in marriage reaches its highest peak experience not when we discover a new technique, find some new romantic getaway spot, or buy just the right lingerie or sexy boxer shorts. The best and highest moments in sex are when we become fully aware of the Presence of God as we become one flesh.

Before we go on to address the characteristics of the Worshipping Heart, we need to address a question you may be asking yourself:

How in the world can you enjoy sex if you know God is watching?

We'd like to answer this question with another question:

How can we possibly enjoy sex unless we know God is watching?

Unless we know that this incredibly private, sacred act is done under the watchful, caring, and approving smile of our Heavenly Father, how can we truly enjoy it?

Yet throughout the centuries, well-meaning theologians and church leaders have wrestled with how to reconcile their spiritual desires with their sexual impulses. Some came to the mistaken conclusion that loving God and enjoying sex were irreconcilable. Therefore, all sexual desires were seen as an enemy to our spiritual growth.

There is even some historical evidence that by the second century A.D., Christians were encouraged to stop having sex after they had produced children. By the Middle Ages, sex was seen primarily for the purpose of procreation and there were even restrictions on which days couples could engage in sexual intercourse—for example, not on feast days, fast days, or Sundays.[9]

Part of the radical divorce between spirituality and sexuality was due not to a careful study of the New Testament and Christ in particular. Rather, it was due to the influence of the secular Greek philosopher Plato, who taught that the material world, including the human body, was hopeless, corrupted, and evil while only the spiritual world was pure and praiseworthy. As his philosophy took hold, even great thinkers such as

---

9. https://www.huffingtonpost.com/entry/christianity-and-sex_
us_56cb6dc1e4b0ec6725e371d5

Augustine taught sexual desire and passion, even within marriage, was inferior to the spiritual life and therefore to be resisted.

The Difference Between Lust and Love

Let's be clear: the Bible clearly condemns lust, sensuality, and immoral behavior. But it does not condemn sexual desire, sexual attraction, or the sexual union within the sacred confines of marriage. If this wasn't the case, books such as the Song of Songs would have to be ripped from the pages of Scripture. The Bible teaches us sex is intended for far more than simply procreation or keeping the human race alive. It is to enjoy almost indescribable pleasure, ecstasy, and satisfaction.

The Bible teaches us sex is intended for far more than simply procreation or keeping the human race alive.

In fact, Scripture teaches, God Himself designed the onset of puberty for a male and female to begin experiencing sexual attraction to one another.

For example, as we noted in the previous chapter, God uses this coming of age attraction as an analogy. In the sixteenth chapter of Ezekiel is a vivid description of the sexual development of a woman from infancy through puberty and beyond. The prophet describes God's love and attraction to the people of Israel, beginning with their birth as a nation. His desire toward them was not for sexual purposes, of course, but for them to be faithful to Him; He would then receive their pure, unadulterated worship.

So it was God, Scripture tells us, who created this overpowering desire and amazing capacity to unite our bodies in physical intimacy in marriage. The Bible clearly teaches, *"For in Him all things were created: things in heaven and on earth, visible and invisible, whether thrones or powers or rulers or authorities; all things have been created through him and for Him"* (Colossians 1:16). "All things" includes the gift of our sexuality and the act of married physical intimacy.

The truth is our Father and Creator *does* know what a married couple are up to in their bedroom, whether they realize it or not. If they are obedient to Him, He smiles upon them with a heavenly benediction. The mystery involved in marriage and the sexual union is so deep and profound, it can only be compared to the mystery of the relationship between Christ and the church.

God knows what a married couple are up to in their bedroom, whether they realize it or not.

Negative Soul Bonds

In the act of sexual intimacy, a mysterious soul bond is formed. Beyond just the physical joining of bodies, there is a joining of two hearts and souls. The apostle Paul goes so far as to say, *"Do you not know that he who unites himself with a prostitute is one with her in body? For it is said, The two will become one flesh"* (1 Corinthians 6:16).

Even in the act of fornication, a soul bond is formed, albeit a negative and ungodly one. A man who hires a prostitute on the streets of Amsterdam, Bangkok, or New York is not married to her simply because he had sex with her. It only means they have formed an illicit or negative soul bond. So mysterious and powerful is the sexual act as God created it that we can spiritually bond to people we otherwise have no connection with.

The Worshipping Heart knows marriage is intended to illustrate the loving, intimate, irreversible, and everlasting bond between Christ and the church. Sex becomes a holy and powerful symbol of the oneness that exists between Christ and His bride, the church. Therefore the Worshipping Heart both welcomes and exalts the Presence of God in the act of married sexual intimacy.

God Is Familiar with All Our Ways, Including Sex

The psalmist rejoiced in the fact that God was a part of each moment of our lives in real time. *"You know when I sit and when I rise; you perceive my thoughts from afar. You discern my going out and my lying down; you are familiar with all my ways. Before a word is on my tongue you know it completely, O Lord…such knowledge is too wonderful for me, too lofty for me to attain"* (Psalm 139:2–6). God's complete and all-inclusive awareness of every moment of our hour of our life includes our life of physical intimacy with our spouse.

It was God's command for a husband and a wife to "become one flesh."

The Worshipping Heart remembers it was God's command for a husband and a wife to "become one flesh." This charge is repeated three times in Scripture. (See Genesis 2, Matthew 19, and Ephesians 5.) There is no mistaking that God designed sex, made it an inseparable part of marriage, and commanded married couples to engage in it as an illustration of the intimate relationship between Christ and the church.

Despite the clear biblical teaching that worshipping God and engaging in sexual intimacy with your spouse are not at odds with each other, doubts remain for many Christians. How can they be holy and pure in God's sight, yet engage regularly in joyous, free-flowing sexual ecstasy in marriage?

Some struggle with the thought, "God is so holy and sexual intercourse seems so fleshly, so downright carnal. The fact I enjoy it as much as I do bothers me. Doesn't the Bible clearly condemn all fleshly desires?"

The Bible does indeed condemn fleshly desires and behavior, saying we are to crucify our flesh. This would appear to be proof positive that all sex is wrong because it apparently feeds our flesh. But the "flesh" it is referring to is our sinful and corrupted human nature, not the physical bodies God created that are made of flesh. To borrow a phrase from Mark Twain, the two terms are as different as a lightning bug is from a lightning bolt.

Christians sometimes confuse "becoming one flesh" with "living according to the flesh" because the same word has two meanings. Becoming one flesh refers to the act of physical intimacy in marriage while the "flesh" the Bible condemns refers to our fallen human nature that selfishly seeks its own way and proudly rebels against God's will and desire for our lives.

A Command Given in the Age of Man's Innocence

God gave us the command to become "one flesh" before sin even entered the world, not afterward. The Bible says, *Adam and his wife were both naked and they felt no shame* (Genesis 2:25). The Bible tells us of God's design for humanity before Adam and Eve took a bite of the forbidden fruit and our human nature became corrupt:

> *So God created mankind in His own image, in the image of God he created them; male and female He created them. God blessed them and said to them, "Be fruitful and increase in number; fill the earth and subdue it."*   (Genesis 1:27–28)

Even an elementary understanding of sexuality includes the knowledge that children are born as the result of the sexual union between a man and a woman. Mankind could not possibly obey the command to "be fruitful and multiply" unless they were to also engage in sexual intercourse.

The classic wedding vows found in the Book of Common Prayer[10] recognizes this command to engage in sexual intimacy was given before sin entered the world:

> "Dearly beloved, we are gathered together here in the sight of God, and in the face of this congregation, to join together this Man and this Woman in holy Matrimony; which is an honorable estate, instituted of God **in the time of man's innocency...**"

The Worshipping Heart knows God is watching when a couple lovingly engages in sexual intimacy. Therefore, if their desire is to honor and please God in every arena of their lives, they must include their sexual lives as well. Rather than seeking to fulfill their own proud desires and engage in selfish sensuality, they seek to bring glory to God every hour of every day of their lives. Even if you know no one else is watching, know that God is.

We're reminded of the French sculptor Frédéric-Auguste Bartholdi, who designed the Statue of Liberty. He paid attention to the smallest

---

10. http://www.pemberley.com/janeinfo/compraym.html

details, even perfectly coiffuring the statue's hair. Why was this so extraordinary? Because in the 1880s, when there were no helicopters, airplanes or satellites to view the top of Lady Liberty, only Bartholdi knew what no one could see from below was done right from above.

In the same way, the Worshipping Heart knows that even when our bedroom door is closed here on earth below, God can see what's going on from heaven above. When engaging in sexual intimacy with your spouse, invite the Presence of God into your marriage and the marriage bed. It can take sexual intimacy to a new level you've never experienced.

Love and Honor Have No Shades of Gray

So how do we bring the awareness and the exaltation of the Presence of Christ into our life of married sexual intimacy? Apostle Paul provides us with some answers we can implement in our marriages starting today:

> *Wives, submit yourselves to your own husbands as you do to the Lord. For the husband is the head of the wife as Christ is the head of the church, his body, of which he is the Savior. Now as the church submits to Christ, so also wives should submit to their husbands in everything. Husbands, love your wives, just as Christ loved the church and gave himself up for her to make her holy, cleansing her by the washing with water through the word, and to present her to himself as a radiant church, without stain or wrinkle or any other blemish, but holy and blameless. In this same way, husbands ought to love their wives as their own bodies. He who loves his wife loves himself. After all, no one ever hated their own body, but they feed and care for their body, just as Christ does the church—for we are members of his body. "For this reason a man will leave his father and mother and be united to his wife, and the two will become one flesh." This is a profound mystery—but I am talking about Christ and the church.* (Ephesians 5:22–32)

As we have noted, husbands and wives must realize everything you do behind bedroom doors is to honor the example of Christ and the church. Anything that would be unloving or dishonoring toward one another must be avoided and forsaken. If we're not sure if a particular sexual act would be pleasing to God and exalt His Presence, simply stop and ask, "Is this behavior an act of redeeming love or extraordinary honor? Is this the way Christ would treat His bride or vice versa?"

Redemptive and holy love is the standard by which we are to evaluate all of our sexual behavior.

Redemptive and holy love is the standard by which we are to evaluate all of our sexual behavior toward our spouses. Is it sacrificial, unselfish love that seeks to bring them closer to God? Is it modeled after the love Christ demonstrated when He went to the cross to redeem us?

To get practical, should Christians watch movies such as *Fifty Shades of Gray* and the sequels? Should they mimic the behavior depicted in these? Reviewers tell us these films detail sadomasochistic sexual behavior intended to produce a twisted sexual high. This doesn't sound like the main characters are seeking to display redeeming love or extraordinary honor, does it? No, it is a glorification of perversion and degradation masquerading as a love story.

Fasting and Prayer Can Change Your Neighborhood

The Worshipping Heart can help you in many aspects of your life, not just your sex life.

A young family lived in a difficult urban neighborhood, across the street from a crack house, a haven for drug dealers, coke-heads, and various criminal types. The noise coming from this house would awaken them in the middle of the night. Menacing German Shepherds roamed the streets to keep rival drug dealers away. Guns were fired into the air when the crack house decided to "celebrate" special occasions like the Fourth of July. The children could not play in their own backyard.

As time went on, the residents of the drug house became more emboldened. They threw empty liquor bottles onto their neighbors' lawns. They broke into people's cars to sit inside and smoke marijuana. Crack house visitors routinely yelled obscenities at the young couple as they carried groceries into their home. Efforts to alert law enforcement did little to stop the activities. The police would usually arrive just after the unsavory clientele had dispersed.

It was early in this couple's marriage—and they reached their breaking point. Rather than retaliating against the lawless neighbors, they decided to take their case to the highest court possible: the court of Heaven, where God reigns as the just Judge of all the earth. They decided to fast until the unbearable situation was finally resolved. They did not know how long it would take. But utilizing their Worshipping Hearts was their last chance for freedom from this nightmare.

One day of fasting went by, then two. They started to feel hunger pangs but soldiered on. They assaulted the gates of heaven with prayer and fasting to bring this neighborhood nightmare to an end. After forty-eight hours of fasting, there was still no change in the activities across the street.

"Do you think we should give up?" the wife asked. "Maybe God has a different plan."

"No, we are not stopping this fast until there is a break in the darkness we are facing," her husband calmly replied.

On the afternoon of the third day, the wife looked out the window and saw something unusual happening across the street. There were two police cars parked outside, then three, four, and finally eight cars lined the street. Some large-scale police operation was under way. Then a police negotiating team walked up the steps and entered the crack house.

Within an hour, several men in their twenties and thirties emerged in handcuffs and were led to a police paddy wagon. A large yellow police tape cordoned off the entire area. Before the day was over, the drug den was thoroughly searched, suspected contraband was confiscated, and finally the entire premises was permanently locked down with a posted warning that no one was to enter.

Without a single shot being fired, the power of fasting and prayer driven by the Worshipping Heart broke the power of criminals who had plagued the neighborhood with drugs and gang activity.

Three Ways Spouses Can Show Redeeming Love

To understand the nature of redemptive love for the Worshipping Heart, let's look at three practical means by which it can be lived out in our marriages on a daily basis:

1. Choose sexual unselfishness as a way of life.

The Bible says, *"Husbands, love your wives, just as Christ loved the church and gave himself up for her"* (Ephesians 5:25). In simple terms, this means asking, "Am I having sex to please myself or to please my spouse first and foremost?"

If you experience climax quickly and leave your spouse unsatisfied, how loving is that?

Let's look at one practical application of this principle. If you experience climax quickly and leave your spouse unsatisfied, how loving is that? Regardless of your spouse's state of arousal, to climax and forget them is incredibly selfish. They will be left feeling disappointed, maybe degraded, and believe you don't care about them. If they are still aroused and you turn over and drift off to sleep, they may be angry, too.

The Worshipping Heart knows Jesus put love for His church before His own needs. In fact, the apostle Paul describes the self-giving nature of the life of Jesus:

> *Who, being in very nature God, did not consider equality with God something to be used to his own advantage; rather, he made himself nothing by taking the very nature of a servant, being made in human likeness.*　(Philippians 2:6–7)

Note that Jesus, though equal with the Father, never used this status to His own advantage. *"Rather, He made himself nothing..."*

Some Bible translations say Jesus *"emptied Himself..."* What did Jesus empty Himself of? Certainly not His divine power or deity or identity. No, He only emptied Himself of the right to use His power, identity or deity for any self-serving purpose. Jesus never turned water into wine because He wanted to taste a fine Chardonnay. He did not multiply the pieces of fish and loaves of bread because it would save Him a walk into town. He did not calm the storm on the Sea of Galilee because He felt seasick.

No, every single act of divine power resulting in a miracle was for someone else's benefit. Jesus never did anything His entire life strictly for His own benefit. This is the example husbands are to follow in loving their wives both inside and outside the bedroom.

The Worshipping Heart realizes that the spouse's need for a climax must be satisfied, regardless of how long you may have to wait to experience one yourself. Applying the words of the apostle Paul to the sexual relationship:

> *Do nothing out of selfish ambition or vain conceit. Rather, in humility value others above yourselves, not looking to your own interests but each of you to the interests of the others. In your relationships with one another, have the same mindset as Christ Jesus.* (Philippians 2:3–5)

When your spouse knows your first priority is to satisfy their sexual needs, they will ultimately come to admire, respond to, and even reciprocate such caring, unselfish love. Requests for sexual intimacy will likely be met with enthusiasm.

2. Choose purity as a way of life.

The apostle Paul goes to great lengths to explain the goal of holy, pure, and redemptive love:

> *To make her holy, cleansing her by the washing with water through the word, and to present her to himself as a radiant church, without stain or wrinkle or any other blemish, but holy and blameless.*
> (Ephesians 5:26–27)

On the other hand, a spouse who is self-focused or full of self-love can easily welcome immoral behavior entering their life.

Ray and Charise (not their real names) came to us for help. Ray was caught using Instagram, Snapchat, and other forms of social media to send photos of himself to his online girlfriend. Charise eventually discovered the sexting and was ready to divorce Ray.

This couple went through our intense, five-day pastoral care program to try to save their marriage. Eventually, Ray came to understand that his mother's death when he was a child left him with a broken heart and led him to seek self-medication through moral failure. Ray was using sexual sin to try to cover his pain of loneliness and grief. Of course, this only produced more pain, as sin always does.

Ray received healing for his broken heart from the precious promise of the Word of God that Jesus had gone to heaven to prepare a place for his mother. Someday, they will be reunited when Christ brings Ray into His Father's House. (See John 14:1–3.) Ray was reassured that he would see his mother again and they would live together for all eternity. With this promise, his life-long pain gradually disappeared.

Charise described the most unexpected result of Ray's repentance from adultery and the healing of his broken heart: "He now reads the Bible to me every morning. He never read the Bible or prayed with me our entire marriage before. Now, he never misses a day. I love it!"

To her delight, what Charise discovered is that when a husband has a Worshipping Heart, his first instinct is to unselfishly minister the Word and prayer to his wife. It is what Paul calls *"cleansing her by the washing of the water through the Word"* (Ephesians 5:26).

The moment Ray repented of his sin and took on the heart of Christ for his wife, his priorities changed. Instead of trying please himself, he now put choosing purity as a way of life. Meeting his wife's spiritual needs as well as her sexual needs became his goal.

Beware of the John the Baptist Syndrome

Spiritual women are attracted to spiritual men—and vice versa. They find them almost irresistible, including sexually.

Bob's senior pastor and mentor while he was growing up was the first one to tell him women are often emotionally drawn to spiritual men. Bob met with his mentor over breakfast at least twice a month all throughout his college and seminary years.

One meeting stands out in Bob's memory because of a particularly powerful message his mentor gave him. He was perhaps twenty years old and was enjoying a large, center-cut, cinnamon roll, and scrambled eggs when his pastor, nearly forty years his senior, told him, "Beware, Bobby, of the John the Baptist syndrome."

"What in the world is that?" Bob asked.

"As a pastor, some women will be turned on by your spirituality," he said. "Be particularly careful if you become a minister. It's not you they will find attractive but what you represent—and they will want that."

Bob nearly choked on his scrambled eggs. Yet he never forgot his wise pastor's advice. Indeed, we have seen many pastors fall in to moral compromise because they were too flattered by a woman's attention. Too late, they came to realize it was actually her desire for a spiritual leader drawing her to him.

Herodias, the illicit wife of Herod, may or may not have been attracted to John the Baptist, but his preaching enraged her, so she had him beheaded. In the thirty-ninth chapter of Genesis, Potiphar's wife was so smitten with Joseph that she asked him many times to have sexual relations with her. Finally, she assaulted him, tearing at his clothes as he fled from her. Angry and embarrassed, she lied to her husband, claiming Joseph had tried to rape her. Like John the Baptist, Joseph promptly found himself in prison.

Fortunately, we're not likely to be thrown into prison for ministering to our spouse's spiritual needs, but we need to choose purity as a way of life. It will make for a lifetime of joyful and satisfying sex with your spouse.

3. Choose nurture as a way of life.

In this same way, husbands ought to love their wives as their own bodies. He who loves his wife loves himself. After all, no one ever hated their own body, but they feed and care for their body, just as Christ does the church—for we are members of his body.   (Ephesians 5:28)

We can show holy, pure, and redemptive love by being considerate of our spouse's spiritual, emotional, and physical needs and nurturing them.

Does your spouse need something from the store? You could offer to go. Is your spouse's brother struggling in his marriage and this is burdening their heart? You can turn off your iPhone, sit down, and listen to their concerns, or even take your brother-in-law out to lunch and offer him some encouragement. Is your spouse tired or has their job been super demanding lately? Change your plans to help with the kids or the household chores so they can find some much needed rest.

Five Signs You Aren't Taking Care of Yourself

1. Your idea of a day at the spa is watching the beautiful colors cascade over you in the car wash.

2. You pretend you are in a flight simulator while sitting in the chair that takes your blood pressure at the drugstore.

3. You tell everyone you're on the Mediterranean diet because you ordered a gyro sandwich at the mall food court.

4. Your vitamin B12 count registered so low even the doctor had no energy to read the results.

5. The last time your name was in lights, it was on the ticket the trooper was handing you as blue and red flashed behind him.

On an airplane, the flight attendant tells us that if something happens and the oxygen masks drop down, we are to put on our own masks first, then help others with theirs. If you are neglecting yourself, you can't take care of your spouse, your family, or your friends. Find the wisdom, determination, and energy to make time for yourself. Ask for help if you need it.

Pay close attention to your spouse. Are they taking care of themselves? If not, step in and do something to give them the relief and renewal their body and soul desperately need. Jesus knows the needs of His church and nurtures her because He is constantly watching, listening, and caring for her.

Lack of Tenderness Is a Turn Off

Some people completely set aside their spouses' need for nurture and think only of their need for sex. One woman we worked with returned home reluctantly after a month-long, painful separation in their marriage due to his anger and controlling behavior. Instead of welcoming her home with a dozen roses and an apology, he virtually attacked her sexually the moment she walked in the door. Having watched pornography while she was gone, he had convinced himself that a forceful sexual encounter would turn her on and restore their relationship. You can only imagine the devastating impact of his twisted and abusive behavior on their marriage.

What if he had met her at the door with flowers instead and sat down on the couch next to her holding her hand. Looking into her eyes, he could have said, "I've been so selfish and unkind. It has so often been all about just what I wanted. I have failed to listen to what you need. Will you forgive me and allow us to start over?"

That night could have ended in bed with a memorable reconciliation. How different the impact on her heart if he had chosen the route of loving nurture over pressure.

The Worshipping Heart is expressed in holy, pure, and redemptive love that chooses the way of unselfishness, produces purity, and provides nurture. All three of these ways of expressing love will positively impact a couple's life of sexual intimacy.

Showing Extraordinary Honor

In what is admittedly one of the more controversial and often-debated portions of Scripture, the apostle Paul writes, "*Wives, submit yourselves to your own husbands as you do to the Lord. For the husband is the head of the wife as Christ is the head of the church, his body, of which he is the Savior. Now as the church submits to Christ, so also wives should submit to their husbands in everything*" (Ephesians 5:22–24).

*Show your spouse the same high regard, respect,
and esteem the church shows for Christ.*

When understood in its proper context and applied to the Worshipping Heart, what Paul is advising can be summed up this way: show your spouse extraordinary honor. Show them the same high regard, respect, and esteem the church shows for Christ.

In the 1990s, a study done by the University of Chicago discovered the one group of women most likely to report satisfaction with their sex lives were conservative, Protestant women.[11] Why? Because they believe in the "holiness" of sex and see it as a means of expressing their love for their husbands.

Offering Worthship

We get the word "worship" from the old English word "worthship," meaning the condition of being worthy or deserving, or having worthiness. When the church of Christ gathers on a Sunday to sing praise choruses and hymns, preach and teach the congregation, receive an offering, celebrate the Lord's table, share a personal testimony, offer prayers, and recite liturgies and creeds, it all has one supreme purpose—to ascribe worth to our Lord and Savior.

Many Eat Fried Chicken and Some Are Saved

Cheryl says, "Bob and I graduated from seminary in 1980, the same year as the Marielitos Cuban boatlift. An estimated 125,000 Cubans reached the United States in seven months, between April and October. By 1982, these Cubans, many of them incarcerated criminals or mental health patients, had been dispersed to various cities across the United States.

"At the time, we were pastoring an inner city church in Minneapolis and team teaching the Twenty/Thirtysomethings Adult Sunday School Class. In class, our Cuban students started sharing that they had been in prison for felonies, in some cases murder, and Castro's officials let them out and put them on boats to the United States. For them, you can imagine, it was a real surprise.

---

11. Robert T. Michael, John H. Gagnon, Edward O. Laumann, *Sex in America, A Definitive Survey* (Boston: Little, Brown, and Company, Inc., 1994)

"I was in the habit of bribing attendees to show up each Sunday to our class with powdered cake doughnuts and bagels. One of the men (ironically named Cocoa) knew the most English and said for breakfast in Cuba, they ate fried chicken, not sweets. From then on, I would get up on Sunday at 6:00 a.m. and cut and fry several chickens for them, believing I was following in a good mission's strategy of embracing the indigenous culture.

"A year later, I was up feeding our new baby Melissa at 2:00 a.m., watching the rerun of the evening news on television to try to stay awake. I couldn't believe it when I saw our most faithful student, Cocoa, being arrested and taken away by the police in front of his apartment, nearby the church, for first degree murder. Cocoa eventually was convicted and sentenced to life in prison. Though he had not responded to the Gospel message, at least he had had the opportunity to hear the Gospel and trusted Christ as his personal Savior in prison.

"We need to go out on a ledge for the Lord, like fixing chicken for felons. The Worshipping Heart seeks to honor Christ's presence both outside our home and inside our marriage. Sharing Christ, even with prisoners and felons, is an act of worship regardless of their response."

Enthusiasm or Boredom?

One way we can show extraordinary honor to our spouse is by communicating that we really enjoy having sex with them and think they're a great lover. A message that we're bored or indifferent will smash their sense of worth.

For some spouses, our wanting to have sex with them and wanting them as a person *are the same thing*. Unfortunately, the opposite is true as well. When we consistently say "no" to our spouse's request for sex and act like it's a burdensome duty on the same level as scrubbing the bathroom fixtures, they feel disrespected. They think if we don't enjoy sex with them, we don't think very highly of them, period.

Falling in Love Is Like Coming to Christ

Extraordinary honor in sexual intimacy can also mean an attitude of submission. Just mentioning the word "submission" can immediately ignite a firestorm of controversy.

*In marriage, you voluntarily yield
your body to your spouse.*

Yet this is a biblical idea repeated numerous times in the New Testament. It means "voluntarily yielding in love." In marriage, you voluntarily yield your body to your spouse. You are naked yet unashamed. You are joined but not embarrassed. You are vulnerable yet secure.

How does a couple get to the point of such vulnerability? How do they go from complete strangers to honoring one another as committed, lifelong, marital lovers, passionately enjoying total sexual knowledge of each other?

They follow a progression of steps—taken in faith and leading to marriage—remarkably similar to how an individual takes steps leading to a saving faith in Jesus Christ. It only makes sense if you believe Paul's Letter to the Ephesians, in which he claims the mystery of marriage resembles that of Christ to the church. Let's look at the process of how a couple meet, fall in love, become engaged, marry, and consummate, and compare this to how an individual hears the message of the Gospel, responds in faith, and comes into a saving relationship with Christ.

Can you identify with this process?

1. Awareness: In romance, God draws our heart to someone who He has chosen for us. In salvation, God draws our heart to Christ, the One He has chosen for us.

2. Conviction: In romance, God convicts us with a strong desire to meet and get to know this person. In salvation, God convicts us with a strong desire to pursue meeting and getting to know Christ.

3. Repentance: In romance, God brings about a profound change of mind and heart toward this person. In salvation, God brings about a profound change of mind and heart toward Christ.

4. Faith: In romance, God creates a willingness in us to trust this person with our heart, life, and future. In salvation, God creates a willingness in us to trust Christ with our heart, life, and future.

5. Invitation: In romance, God gives us the desire to ask this person to share a permanent, intimate, and life-long relationship called marriage. In salvation, God gives us the desire to ask Christ to share a permanent, intimate, and life-long relationship with us called salvation.

6. Commitment: In romance, God empowers us to publicly confess at our wedding our lifelong vows of exclusive love, fidelity, and honor to this person. In salvation, God empowers us to publicly confess at baptism our lifelong vows of exclusive love, fidelity, and honor to Him.

7. Intimacy: In romance, God knits our hearts together in intimate love, knowledge, and submission so we are no longer two, but one. In salvation, God knits our hearts together in intimate love, knowledge, and submission so we are no longer two, but one.

Just as we voluntarily yield to Christ in love when we walk with Him, we voluntarily yield to our mates in married sexual intimacy. The words "submit" and "surrender" are somewhat similar when it comes to relationships. Yet the word "surrender" also has a largely negative connotation in our society. It conjures up images of a defeated general handing his sword to the conquering officer as he then walks away in humiliation, despair, and sorrow.

But surrender in biblical terms means yielding yourself to another person in complete trust, freedom, and abandonment. Think of a happy couple on their honeymoon, lying in each other's arms as they contemplate their future together. They are surrendering to each other in bliss and peace.

E. Stanley Jones, the famous devotional writer of the 1930s, believed that total surrender to Christ was the primary key to finding joy, fulfillment, and power in the Christian life. He wrote a devotional book entitled *Victory through Surrender*[12] that is still in circulation today.

If true, then loving and total surrender in marriage and the sexual act is necessary as well. The Worshipping Heart understands surrender and submission lead to sexual joy, contentment, and fulfillment when we voluntarily yield in love and devotion.

A Lesson in Devotion from a Prodigal Collie

Devotion to one another in marriage is a powerful bonding agent. True devotion—that powerful feeling of love or loyalty—is timeless. Let us use a true story as an illustration.

The only time our family was featured nationally on the morning news had nothing to do with our careers, books we have written, or our personal accomplishments. We landed a guest appearance on the CBS Morning Show, an article in the *Chicago Tribune*, features on several international wire services, and fifteen minutes of fame, all thanks to the family dog, Bo, short for Boaz.

Bo was a purebred Collie that looked remarkably like the universally loved and adored Lassie from the popular television series that ran from the 1950s through the early 1970s.

But Bo was no hero. He was a challenge from the day we brought him home at two months of age. For one thing, he loved to chew our woodwork. He also enjoyed eating entire plates of raw hamburger patties if you happened to walk into the house from the patio, leave both them and Bo outside, even for a minute.

Like a main character from *Prison Break*, he routinely escaped our back yard and ended up in town in the local bookstore, bakery and, finally, the police station. The last landing place cost us a cool seventy-five dollars and a stern lecture from a uniformed official who obviously had not grown up watching *Lassie*.

So how did Bo get us on the front page of several newspapers? Simple. He ran away.

---

12. E. Stanley Jones, *Victory Through Surrender: Self-Realization Through Self-Surrender* (Nashville, TN: Abingdon Press, 1980)

He mysteriously disappeared one Memorial Day from our backyard. After several months and then years of searching for him, we gave up. Our Collie was either lost or dead. We had abandoned all hope of seeing him again until five years later—yes, five years—when we received a call one summer morning from an animal shelter some seventy-five miles from our suburb in Chicago. They had Bo in custody.

"That's impossible," we stammered into the phone. "Bo has been gone over five years."

"It's definitely Bo and you can come and pick him up," said the dispatcher at the dog pound. Bo still had the microchip we had implanted under his skin when he was a puppy. When a neighbor in Rockford, Illinois, called to report a mangy looking dog going through her garbage, the animal control people were sent out and quickly apprehended Bo.

While not subjected to paw-printing or a mugshot, Bo nonetheless was given a thorough exam by the county veterinarian. When Bo's back was scanned, the computer screen popped up with the message, "Reported missing."

Bo had primarily belonged to our son, Brent, when he was fifteen years old. Now, twenty-two and working at a corporate office, Brent made the seventy-five-mile journey with us to get the Prodigal Puppy. As we drove to the animal shelter, it was still too much to believe that Bo was alive some five years after his disappearance.

Once we arrived at the shelter, we were warned not to rush toward Bo or try to hug him. "He might not remember you," intoned the unit captain. "He could bite you."

Bo was on an orange leash as he was brought out from around a corner. He stopped for a moment and stared at us. His hair was matted, his paws were dirty, and he was covered with briars from years of living in the wild. But the moment he saw Brent, he ran toward our son. He jumped up, paws first, and proceeded to lick Brent's face. Even the captain of the animal control unit, who looked remarkably like legendary tough guy Chicago Bears Coach Mike Ditka, was seen wiping tears from his eyes.

Few words can describe the memorable reunion between Brent and his Bo. What sums it up best is "devotion." After years of separation, hardship, and no doubt near starvation, Bo was still filled with love and loyalty for Brent. A news reporter was present and recorded their tearful reunion on camera. The footage was sent out—and created a media firestorm. We returned home that afternoon to find an ABC News satellite truck parked in our driveway. For the next three days, the Moeller dog miracle story went viral.

Devotion enables us to weather difficult circumstances, long separations, and even the possibility of death.

There is something about the quality of devotion that touches human hearts. This rare trait enables us to weather difficult circumstances, long separations, and even the possibility of death, and still remain completely and entirely attracted, committed, and loyal to another. This is why it's often called "undying" devotion.

It is this trait of the Worshipping Heart that so resembles Christ and the church. How does our devotion play out in our marriage in every day terms? Are other members of the opposite sex interested in us? Fugetaboutit! Is our spouse suddenly unemployed and can't provide for the family? It doesn't matter. We remain committed to them. Does a health problem prevent our spouse from being intimate with us? That doesn't change our mind. We still love them.

There is a reason we often refer to our time spent alone with God, reading His Word, and praying as our "devotions." We ascribe love, loyalty, and worth to our Savior with the time we devote exclusively to deepening our relationship with Him.

The Worshipping Heart knows there are few other activities in marriage that can so beautifully express the power of devotion to one another as sexual intercourse. No one else on earth experiences what we do with our spouse. No one else gains such an intimate knowledge of who they are.

No one else shares the exquisite moments we do with our one and only marital partner.

When a spouse submits and surrenders themselves in sexual intimacy, such amazing devotion can ignite true joy.

Counterfeits of the Worshipping Heart

We'd like to offer a few notes of caution regarding the counterfeits to the Worshipping Heart that some couples sadly settle for or allow in their marriage. Two are particularly troubling, if not dangerous, to married sexual intimacy.

1. The Idolatrous Heart

This heart focuses entirely on worshipping the creature rather than the Creator. The emphasis shifts from centering on heart-to-heart intimacy to simply body-to-body performance. The Idolatrous Heart begins to evaluate and critique how good or bad the spouse is as a sexual companion. Performance replaces acceptance and pleasure replaces love. Achieving the strongest sexual climax or sustaining the sexual act as long as possible becomes the ultimate goal of the encounter. It is sex for the sake of sex—and little else.

The Idolatrous Heart begins to evaluate and critique how good or bad the spouse is as a sexual companion.

The apostle Paul warns against this subtle shift from worshipping the Creator to worshipping the creature:

> *For although they knew God, they neither glorified him as God nor gave thanks to him, but their thinking became futile and their foolish hearts were darkened....They exchanged the truth about God for a lie and worshiped and served created things rather than the Creator—who is forever praised.* (Romans 1:21, 25)

Much has been written already about this solemn warning in Romans and where sex for its own sake can eventually lead. Suffice it to say without the Worshipping Heart, the sexual act in marriage can quickly descend into the worship of the idol of sex for its own sake and all the sad degradation and devaluation that soon follows.

2. The Carnal Heart

The Carnal Heart is drawn to the worship of pleasure for its own sake.

The Carnal Heart is drawn to the worship of pleasure for its own sake. We must remember that pleasure is only as virtuous, edifying, legitimate, and holy as the object it draws us to. Listening to a beautiful music performance in a park on a warm summer's night can be a marvelous pleasure if it leads us to praise the God who created harmony and melody. Eating a delicious meal with family and friends during the holidays can be pure pleasure if it draws us to remember the God who provides for all our needs. Enjoying an exquisite hour of sexual intimacy with our spouse can be one of life's most delicious moments if we acknowledge Christ as the Author of love.

Just as there are legitimate pleasures in life, there are illegitimate ones as well. Drunkenness may produce enjoyable "good times," but the pain it causes in the hearts of children, family, and friends of alcoholics is far from pleasant. Some drugs reportedly produce a feeling of euphoria, but they often lead to crime, violence, and cruelty, bringing others intense sorrow. Pornography gives its own sense of perverse, momentary pleasure, but the anguish it creates in a marriage is bitter beyond measure.

Here are some manifestations of the Carnal Heart that should be rejected: incest, sexual abuse or rape; pornography of all types, including Internet sites, videos, magazines, movies, and television; cyber-sex and virtual reality sex; homosexuality; anal sex; adultery and "wife swapping"; indecent exposure or voyeurism; bestiality; prostitution; visiting topless bars or strip clubs; and sexual harassment.

Some may think a few of the aforementioned behaviors are acceptable for a married couple, but we disagree. Our study of Scripture leads us to believe there is no place for these carnal practices in a godly marriage.

The Carnal Heart can become an addiction that turns us to extreme self-focus. We may come to the point where we will do anything we need to do in order to experience that sexual high over and over again. It can drive us to impose our selfish lust on our spouse regardless of their emotional needs or well-being at the moment. It can reduce the marriage bed to little more than a location for the self-focused release of sexual tensions, minus any meaningful communication or heart connection. How much pleasure we personally experience becomes the only standard by which we evaluate our sexual intimacy.

Without the Worshipping Heart,
sex is practiced for its own sake.

Without the Worshipping Heart, sex is practiced for its own sake. There is no transcendent awareness of God, just the physical gratification of the moment. When we are in love with sensuality and eroticism rather than with our spouse's heart and mind, it ultimately reduces us to servitude and bondage.

By What Standard?

If God is not present in our lives, marriage and bedroom, by what standard are we to measure our sexual behavior? Is the only standard for your sexual conduct what the two of you are willing to agree to? If you both agree watching pornography or engaging in some other activity is a way to achieve new levels of arousal, does that make it right?

As Christians, we cannot afford to bury our heads in the sand like ostriches and hope sexual perversions disappear. They are here—and they are getting worse.

The HBO series *Westworld*, which premiered in 2016, imagines a future in which people interact with life-like "hosts" in a vast amusement park. The guests are welcome to do everything they please with these humanoid robots, from "killing" them to using them for sex.

The future is here. A 2017 report by the research firm YouGov (today. yougov.com) found that 24 percent of American men (and 9 percent of women) would consider having sex with a robot. In the United Kingdom, the owner of one such device has "introduced" it to his children as part of the family.

It gets worse: some robots have been built to resemble children. In response, the U.S. Congress introduced the Curbing Realistic Exploitative Electronic Pedophilic Robots (CREEPER) bill to ban their importation.

Of course, none of these robots have minds, hearts, or souls—but maybe that's the point. Used impurely for self-gratification, they can only be the work of the devil. The Worshipping Heart wants nothing to do with them.

How can we know if some particular sexual act or behavior promotes the Worshipping Heart or counterfeits it? Again, there is a relatively simple test to employ: Does what we are thinking about doing with our mate convey genuine unselfish love and extraordinary honor? Or does it primarily feed our self-focused desire for pleasure, even at the cost of degrading our hearts and bodies?

God's Word gives us some general instructions about what activity should occur in the bedroom.

God's Word gives us some general instructions about what activity should occur in the bedroom and what should not. (See the Song of Songs, Romans 1.) For the most part, however, we are left to deduce such things from the general principles of sacrificial love and extraordinary honor. The Bible teaches us we are to honor God in all that we do, seek the ultimate goal of love, practice self-control, and keep the marriage bed pure.

While this may seem to limit our sexual behavior in marriage, we need to remember that one day, we shall give an account to God of everything we have done on earth. Yes, including what has happened between the sheets. *"For we must all appear before the judgment seat* of Christ, so that each of us may receive what is due us for the things done while in the body, whether good or bad"* (2 Corinthians 5:10).

On the other hand, if you think, somehow, God is against all of the exquisite pleasures and ecstasy married sex can produce, we ask you to stay tuned for our upcoming chapter on the Ecstatic Heart.

Caring for the Worshipping Heart

Let's look at some practical ways we may lovingly nurture and care for the Worshipping Heart in our sexual relationship.

First, be willing to spend time in prayer and Bible prior to and after the experience of sexual intimacy. Like Bob's roommate in college who began his honeymoon with a deep, sincere time of prayer, let us remember to allow meaningful spiritual intimacy to precede meaningful physical intimacy.

Make the goal of your sexual encounter to show love and honor to God and one another.

Next, make the goal of your sexual encounter to show love and honor to God and one another. As you honor God, you will be honoring one another as well.

Finally, ask God to display the fruit of the Spirit in your life of sexual intimacy. Is how I approach my spouse to ask for sex filled with love, joy, peace, patience, kindness, and goodness? Is how I respond to my spouse's request equally Spirit-filled? Are my attitudes and actions during the act of sexual intimacy displaying the fruit of the Spirit? When the results of the sexual encounter are sometimes less than satisfying, do I still display the fruit of the Spirit?

Evangelist and author James Robison once said, "For a long while, I practiced the gifts of the Spirit without displaying the fruit of the Spirit."

Perhaps the same thing can be said when it comes to our life of sexual intimacy. Perhaps our gifts or strengths as a lover are on full display, but do we show the fruit of the Spirit, controlled, directed, and motivated by love?

Some time ago, we met a pastor who had undergone surgery for prostate cancer. While the procedure saved his life, it left him unable to perform sexually. "Yes, I miss that aspect of our marriage," his wife admitted. "But we still have great times together. I thank God every day I still have him." That's true sacrificial love and extraordinary honor.

It would be difficult to describe the devotion of the Worshipping Heart in any better terms.

Questions to Consider:

1. Why do many people believe having sex with your spouse is something completely separate from worshipping God?

2. Should the idea that God is watching all our behavior—including our sexual behavior—be a distressing thought or a comforting one?

3. Why are redeeming love and extraordinary honor important to fulfilling sexual intimacy in marriage?

God's Word to Consider:

"On the third day a wedding took place at Cana in Galilee. Jesus' mother was there, and Jesus and his disciples had also been invited to the wedding....and the master of the banquet tasted the water that had been turned into wine....This, the first of his miraculous signs, Jesus performed in Cana of Galilee. He thus revealed his glory, and his disciples put their faith in him." (John 2:1–2; 9; 11)

4

THE COMPANION HEART

Then the LORD *God made a woman from the rib He had taken out*
of the man, and He brought her to the man. The man said,
"This is now bone of my bones and flesh of my flesh; she shall be called
'woman,' for she was taken out of man."
For this reason a man will leave his father and mother and be united
to his wife and they will become one flesh.
—Genesis 2:22–24

The Companion Heart gives and receives love through deep soul-ties,
emotional camaraderie, and undying loyalty.

> *If you live life as close friends,*
> *then sex will only deepen your bond.*

A recent study from the National Bureau of Economic Research found
that people who consider their spouses to be their best friends get almost
twice as much life satisfaction from marriage than other couples.[13] It

---

13. http://www.nber.org/papers/w20794

stands to reason, then, that if you want your spouse to be your best friend, you need to do things together.

Bob took this idea to heart one day and asked Cheryl to go goose-hunting with him. In those days, the great, gray, majestic Canadian geese flew in V-formations, honking wildly (perhaps their own form of road rage) as they soared high above the earth in the moonlight. Today, all you have to do to encounter a goose is go to your local library or park, where you will find gaggles of geese milling about on the sidewalk, totally oblivious to your presence. (Do be careful not to wear your best shoes.)

But in those days, bagging the splendid gray goose was considered a rare prize.

"You're really going to enjoy this," Bob said with a grin. "We'll get up at 3:00 a.m., drive in the dark to the border of the state game refuge, and by sunrise, we'll start blasting away."

Cheryl nodded. "Sure, I've always wanted to watch the sunrise with you."

"With my sharp aim and steady eye, I'll get you a new goose down pillow," Bob promised.

Soon the chilly, November day arrived. Bob excitedly nudged Cheryl awake from her deep sleep. Already fully awake and brimming with energy, he said, "Hey, can you believe it? It's 3:00 a.m. This is it! Let's go." Cheryl dragged herself out of bed.

We drove across the western Minnesota prairie in the dark. Bob wanted to get there early to secure the best "pit" to hide in. To him, the damp, pre-dawn marsh with five-foot-tall cattail plants, barren trees, and deep holes in the ground for blinds all resembled the Garden of Eden.

Bob grinned as he looked around in the fog. "It must have been a place just like this that Adam and Eve became best friends."

As we settled into our marsh pit, Bob's Companion Heart beat thunderously inside his chest. He thought, "Here I am. I have my twelve-gauge shotgun. I have my Thermos of hot coffee. And I have my babe sitting right next to me. Does life get any better than this?"

After dawn, the growing cacophony of honking indicated the first formation of geese was headed our way. As they soared overhead, traveling at nearly fifty miles an hour, Bob sprang to his feet. He took aim at the lead goose and unleashed a fusillade of steel shotgun pellets. In no time at all, Bob had emptied all three shells he was legally allowed to fire under the game refuge's rules before having to exit the marsh.

Now, we want to reassure any animal rights activists and our Canadian friends that no geese were injured that day. In fact, in all of Bob's years of goose hunting, he never hit a single one.

Well, there was the time he was playing golf on our local par-three course and accidentally bonked a sleeping goose on the head with a ball on the fairway. But that one, too, lived to honk the tale.

No, the only goose that was cooked that fateful November day we went hunting was Bob's. While Cheryl loves all things outdoors, it *was* the middle of the night, below freezing, wet, and muddy. And we had to dodge messy aerial gifts from the geese. However, the excursion definitely did something for our Companion Hearts—exactly what is still under discussion.

The Friendless American Husband

In study after study, most men admit they don't have a single close friend. They may have buddies they "do stuff" with, but no one to talk to about their feelings, fears, or insecurities. Most women, on the other hand, have close, satisfying relationships with many people—friends, neighbors, family members, coworkers, a group at church, and others.

Perhaps this is one reason why widows seem to cope better with the loss of their mates than widowers. Throughout their lives, they have built a variety of relationships, giving them an emotional support system to help to fill the void left by their husbands' passing. It's a very different story for husbands. As a pastoral couple, we have seen the near total emotional devastation that occurs when a man loses his wife.

Decades ago, an article in a women's magazine did a study of divorced men who were going to remarry. The number one characteristic that attracted them to their new wives? "They are my best friend."

One marriage counselor often asks the husband in his office, "Would you rather feel close to your wife and enjoy emotional intimacy, or would you rather have sexual intimacy with her?" The overwhelming majority of men, he reports, say they would prefer to feel an emotional connection to their wives over making love.

Many of the men and women who seek help for their marriages have enjoyed a strong sexual relationship, but they are still frustrated with each other. Spouses drawn into pornography or illicit affairs rarely cite lack of sex with their mates as the cause.

Something else is often missing. They may not always put it into words. Yet when you ask them why they were attracted to a coworker or someone they met on social media, they will say things like, "She listened to me and laughed at my jokes," "He likes the same music I do," "She told me I was really smart," or "He always has time to talk to me."

The common theme in each of these is that the other person gave the spouse an emotional connection. In other words, the cheating spouse found the friend he or she had been looking for.

*True companionship makes for natural
and spontaneous sex.*

Spouses feel comforted when they know we are their life-long companions, filling a need for friendship and erasing any loneliness in their hearts. True companionship makes for natural, spontaneous sex as the two of you truly enjoy each other's company both day and night. The Companion Heart can take a lukewarm sexual relationship and make it sizzle when a husband and wife become what God always intended them to be—the best of friends. Willard Harley, best-selling marriage author, says having a "recreational companion" is one of a husband's most important needs.[14]

14. Willard F. Harley, Jr., *His Needs, Her Needs: Building an Affair-Proof Marriage* (Grand Rapids, MI: Baker Publishing Group, 1986)

Tired of Naming Bugs

You can understand why Adam had the wind knocked out of him when he saw Eve for the first time. After spending months, or perhaps years, naming animals and insects such as the duck-billed platypus, orangutan, and the pleasing fungus beetle (*Erotylidae*), Adam was at a loss for words when he feasted his eyes on the newest member of his own species. The fact that she was the only other member of his species no doubt added to her appeal.

All the astonished Adam managed to say when he first saw Eve in all of her stunning feminine beauty was, *"This is now bone of my bones, and flesh of my flesh; she shall be called 'woman,' for she was taken out of man"* (Genesis 2:23).

Adam's first words may not sound romantic or imaginative. It seems the best he can do is compliment her on their common bone structure and remind her he's the one who donated a rib to the relationship.

Yet, if you dig underneath the somewhat awkward and analytical words, you find something different is going on. Although Adam uses "manspeak," he is actually communicating something from his heart to Eve's heart. He is trying to tell her something more meaningful, mysterious, and arousing than anything William Shakespeare, Jane Austen, or Alfred Lord Tennyson ever penned.

The first characteristic of the Companion Heart is the deep soul-ties that come from believing we are meant for each other for life.

When Adam says Eve is *"bone of my bones, and flesh of my flesh,"* he is confessing that out of all God's wondrous creation, with an endless variety of animals, birds, fish, and other species, she and she alone is meant for him and he for her. Is there anything more satisfying in life than to know the two of you were meant for each other?

Our world often offers incredibly great twosomes: a burger and fries; Monday night and football; campfire and marshmallows; and Christmas and *It's a Wonderful Life*. You know if you get one, you get the other.

But there never were two entities on earth more intended for each other than Adam and Eve. When Adam gazed upon Eve, he proclaimed a new, mysterious, and compelling soul bond unlike anything creation had ever seen.

The Honeymoon Is the Ultimate Discovery Channel

When a married couple knows they are meant for each other, it keeps the fire stoked in their sexual relationship. One of the amazing discoveries of the honeymoon is just how perfectly God created the male and female bodies for each other. Only an infinitely wise and loving Creator could have designed the exhilarating features of the two becoming one. The design of the human body is one of life's more irrefutable arguments that sex was meant to be exclusively the union of a man and a woman.

Beyond the physical evidence that a couple are meant for each other is another amazing honeymoon realization: it's now okay to have sex, free of guilt, shame, and sin. It's a beautiful feeling.

There is deep mystery to the Companion Heart. We now belong sexually to each other not just for this night, or the next, but for the rest of our lives. This unique friendship is unlike any other on earth. Only among married companions is it considered healthy, normal, and godly to sleep in the same bed, view each other's nakedness, and hold and caress each other's bodies whenever the desire or opportunity presents itself. To fail to regularly engage in these actions under normal circumstances is cause to believe the marriage is headed toward serious trouble.

The Labors of True Companionship

Not only is the sexual act a sign of lasting soul-ties, but so are the children produced as a result of such bonded intimacy.

Bob was present for the birth of all of our six children. Each time he held one of our newborns for the first time, he knew he was holding a precious gift given by Cheryl, his best friend on earth. Each time Bob walked out of the delivery room, he would shake his head at the miracle he had just witnessed and ask himself, "How can someone not believe in a Creator God?"

An Important Word

We often wonder how anyone could let a sweet, innocent child be torn from the womb by abortion. After watching the miracle of six live births, we simply cannot understand this cruel and horrible practice. When we contemplate the procedures used to extract an unborn child, we are left dumbfounded, speechless, and heartbroken.

Childbirth beautifully illustrates our love for each other.

Childbirth beautifully illustrates our love for each other. Our intimate companionship has created a new life that is exactly the product of half of each spouse. The wife gives her husband the greatest gift in the world by carrying this new life in her body for nine months and bringing the infant into the world amid much labor and pain. Nothing can top the happiness you feel when you hold your baby for the first time. It is the ultimate soul-tie of two committed lifelong companions.

The Hebrew word for sexual intimacy found in the account of Adam and Eve is the same word that means "to know." The Bible says Adam knew Eve and she bore him a son. The Companion Heart thrives on knowing and being known by our spouses. It creates intimate friendship soul-ties at the deepest level God designed for two people to know. This knowledge continues to build companionship over a lifetime that neither sickness, setbacks, nor tragedy can separate.

Throughout the years, friends have given us many things—good advice, their undivided attention, the courage to keep going when we felt like quitting, and more. But only one friend on earth, my spouse, was so convinced we were meant for each other that we were willing and able to together conceive six children and give the best years of our lives to raising them.

Children have given us much joy, in some unexpected ways. We will never forget the time our son, Andrew, then three years old, attended an evening service with us that included communion. As the ushers passed the plate of cracker wafers down our row, Andrew, who hadn't eaten supper yet, grabbed a big handful of crackers and shoved them all into his mouth. We were horrified, the ushers were incensed, and Andrew was satisfied. Perhaps, in his innocence, he was closer than any of us in understanding the Lord's table is indeed a feast.

Lord Melbourne and the Queen

The Companion Heart is a need everyone carries—even royalty. Consider the story of Queen Victoria and William Lamb, Lord Melbourne, the prime minister of Britain in the early 1800s. Eighteen-year-old Victoria suddenly became queen after the death of her uncle, King William IV. Like most teenagers, she was unprepared, naïve, and impulsive—while taking on the most difficult job in the British Empire.

Lord Melbourne, a widower forty years her senior, was weary of politics and eager to retire to a more private life at his country estate, Brockington Hall. But sensing Victoria's vulnerability and inexperience, he stepped in to become her unofficial advisor and confidante. He artfully helped the teenage queen navigate the treacherous waters of politics, global enemies, and jealous relatives. He patiently tutored her in the rules of effective monarchy and the art of protocol.

Was the young queen in love with the gentle, mannerly, older Lord Melbourne? In her diary, she called him "my kind and excellent Lord Melbourne," later noting, "He has something so fatherly and so affectionate and kind in him, that one must love him."[15]

Although the prime minister was much older than his queen, he likely developed feelings for her as well. He spent hours every day counseling her. In a January 1838 letter to her, he wrote:

"Lord Melbourne feels most deeply the extreme kindness of your Majesty's expressions. Whatever may happen in the course of events, it will always be to Lord Melbourne a source of the most lively satisfaction to have assisted your Majesty in the commencement of your reign, which was not without trouble and difficulty, and your Majesty may depend that whether in or out of office Lord Melbourne's conduct will always be directed by the strongest attachment to your Majesty's person, and by the most ardent desire to promote your Majesty's interests."[16]

Lord Melbourne stayed by Victoria's side throughout the long day of her coronation on June 28, 1838. Afterward, he noted she must be very

---

15. Queen Victoria, *The Girlhood of Queen Victoria: A Selection from Her Majesty's Diaries Between the Years 1832, and 1840* (John Murray, London, 1912)
16. https://archive.org/details/lettersofqueenvi01victuoft

tired, especially considering the weight of the coronation robes and crown. With tears in his eyes, he told her, "And you did it beautifully every part of it, with so much taste."[15]

You could say Lord Melbourne and Queen Victoria shared a Companion Heart.

For some, the Companion Heart brings a level of soul-ties that not even death can sever. When they mate, they mate for life. Bob's grandfather lived as a widower for twenty-eight years after his wife's premature death due to rheumatic fever. "I knew I could never love another woman as much as I loved her," he would explain. "There was no use trying."

The second characteristic of the Companion Heart is the emotional camaraderie that comes from becoming the best of friends.

When Adam gave Eve the name "woman" because she was "taken out of man," he said something both mysterious and beautiful: "Because you were taken out of me, I will forever be incomplete without you."

What is a best friend after all? Isn't it someone you have an emotional bond with? Isn't it someone without whom your life would feel incomplete? Isn't it a belief that we are friends who share the same values, convictions, and faith?

What Good Is a Husband Without a Head?

Cheryl says, "During the middle of one night, I woke for a moment and reached out to pat Bob on the head so I could feel his comforting warmth. But I didn't find his head, so I reached again.

"Failing a second time, I reached with both hands. Not succeeding in finding his head three times, I thought, oh, no, where is Bob's head? I really have always liked his head. This is horrific, what good is a husband without a head? Oh, no, will I be blamed for my headless husband?

"I almost had a heart attack. I leaped backward from the bed and flipped on the light.

"There in front of me was the telling evidence. I didn't know Bob had cleaned out his side of our closet and everything he owned was in huge pile on his side of the bed, packed so close together it resembled a man's body. I had mistaken it for Bob when I went to bed earlier without turning the light on.

"Bob had an explanation for me when I found him on his computer writing in the screened-in gazebo outside. He had read an article about using a writing schedule that allowed for more time in the evening with the kids after dinner before they went to sleep. He had started that new writing schedule without telling me, using the late night hours to write. Bob, my headless husband, was really out using his head.

"The Companion Heart misses their spouse when they're apart. They long to be close to each other as much as possible—head, hands, and heart included."

Warning Label: Don't Try Life Alone

The need for companionship goes back to the Creator's original design, "It is not good for man to be alone…" To paraphrase, "It is extremely difficult to go through life by yourself," or even, "It may be emotionally destructive for you to be alone." This may be why married men and women live longer than their single counterparts.

The need for companionship goes back to the Creator's original design.

Those who ignore their health or have bad habits are especially in need of a mate. Their spouses may encourage them to eat more fresh vegetables or make sure they go in for an annual physical when they'd be content to eat potato chips all day and check their blood pressure at Walmart every five years. A spouse can help them improve their diet and get regular checkups. In caring for them, the spouse is providing vital emotional support and companionship.

Moms Need Each Other, Too

> "Older women likewise are to be reverent in behavior, not slanderers or slaves to much wine. They are to teach what is good, and so train the young women to love their husbands and children."   (Titus 2:3–4)

Cheryl says, "My mom used to have her questions about life, laundry, and children answered as she chatted over the backyard fence while hanging the laundry on the clothesline. If a mom was hanging up her laundry, it was a signal she was available to chat. Younger moms would come by to ask questions such as how to clear up the baby's ear infection, how to use bluing to get the laundry brighter, and why husbands never put the cap back on the tube of toothpaste.

"Today, instead of chatting across the fence, if a mom has time to chat at all, it may be a brief exchange on Facebook, a short conversation at the grocery store, or sixty minutes at a coffee shop. For most moms, this is not enough. The truth is, every mom needs a mom. My mother was far away, so I would always call her or visit when I could.

"But I also always found an older woman I respected who could model mature Christian motherhood in person on a daily basis—a woman like Anna, who walked close to the Lord, in wise ways.

"Anna is mentioned only briefly in Luke 2. She was a prophetess who walked so close to the Lord that when she met Baby Jesus in the temple, she knew who He was without being told. Closeness to the Lord brings about a special sensitivity, one of the best gifts a mom can have. We should be so close to the Lord that we notice when someone is hurting and others see Christ in us.

"Do you have an older godly mom in your life to whom you can turn for counsel when motherhood or marriage has you in a corner? If you're an older mom, are you encouraging a younger mom who needs your wisdom? If your answer is no to either question, ask God to direct you to the mom you need to connect with.

"Although my earthly mom is now in heaven, she left a godly, quiet legacy of love."

The Buddy System Never Grows Old

Did you go to summer camp as a child? If so, you should remember "the buddy system." You learned you never go swimming in the lake or hiking in the woods unless you were always within sight of your buddy. That way, if you went underwater and didn't come back up, or fell and twisted your ankle, your buddy would immediately know and call out or run for help.

The Companion Heart operates much the same way as the Buddy System. If one of us goes under, the other spouse will immediately know and get or provide help. That's what friends do. They keep us afloat through life's sometimes difficult and treacherous currents and storms.

Be Careful What You Pray For

Sometimes, as couples age and they've been married a few years, they go through a "mid-life crisis," thinking they may be missing out on fantastic sex with someone younger than their spouse.

We like the story about a couple who wed when they were both twenty. They had a seemingly happy, harmonious marriage and were now forty-five years old. On the night of their twenty-fifth wedding anniversary, both had the same dream.

In her dream, a shining angel appeared to the wife and said, "Greetings from heaven. I was sent here to tell you how pleased we are to see the strong, committed, and loving marriage you have enjoyed for twenty-five years. I have been authorized to grant you any wish you might desire."

The woman smiled with delight and quickly replied, "We have never travelled to any exotic places and now that we are helping to put our kids through college, we don't have much money. Could we travel the world together?"

"Why, of course," replied the angel. He suddenly flashed his silver sword and blinding light overtook the woman. She awakened to find airline tickets, cruise line reservations, and a package deal of five-star hotels on her nightstand.

The husband had the same dream. The angel told him he could ask for anything. "Well, I hope this doesn't upset anyone up there," he said hesitantly, "but I was wondering if my wife could be twenty years younger."

The angel smiled. "Why, of course," he said, "That's not a problem." He once again flashed his silver sword and the room blazed with light. A moment later, the man woke up and gasped. He was now sixty-five years old.

Design a Day with a Loyal Companion

Actually, we think most people would rather have a good friend—a life-long buddy—rather than a younger, good-looking guy or gal who's only interested in sex. A spouse who enjoys going to sporting events or getting up early on a Saturday morning to go fishing. Someone who likes to go shopping with you or laugh with you over a YouTube video.

Loyal companionship is vital in a marriage. If your spouse is your best friend, enjoys sharing your joys and challenges, and believes in you, you will experience the emotional and sexual benefits of the Companion Heart. If you want to share that heart and increase your sex appeal, add fuel to your intimacy, and be irresistible, ask your spouse what an ideal day spent alone together might look like to him or her—then make it happen.

Ask your spouse what an ideal day spent alone together might look like—then make it happen.

Don't argue. Just go and do it. Let your spouse design twenty-four hours that would bring him or her the most joy, relaxation, and fulfillment, and then make every effort to make their wish come true.

While the answer will vary, a husband might propose something like this:

"What if we wake up early Saturday and have sex? Then let's go to the gym and work out for an hour. We can finish by sitting in the whirlpool for fifteen minutes. After that, let's head over to our favorite breakfast place. Hmmm. Thick sliced bacon, strong coffee, and hashed browns laced with bacon and onions! Then, let's stop by the auto mall and look at the latest cars and pick-ups, then head over to Home Depot to pick up three bags of fertilizer for the lawn. Tonight, we can sit on the couch and watch the baseball playoffs. They start at 6:00 p.m. How about you make your famous chili and pour it over some nacho chips? Then let's have sex again. Would that be a great day or what?"

Now imagine what would happen if the wife's reaction went something like this:

"Well, apart from the sex before breakfast and at the end of the day, why don't you just call your cousin up and spend the day with him? I'm sure he'd be thrilled with your line-up of greasy food, monster trucks that cost a year's wages, and mind-numbing sports broadcasters who argue like the fate of the civilized world is at stake. I might as well go and get a seaweed wrap at the spa. See you at 10:00 p.m. and don't expect too much when I get home. I'll be smelling like Pacific kelp."

This woman fails to understand her husband's need for the Companion Heart. Yes, he could do almost everything on his wish list with one of his relatives or a buddy from work. But he would rather do all of those things with his wife. God created a place in his heart that only she can fill.

Sure, Bob had fun with his friends from college—going on weekend fishing trips, downhill skiing in the winter, and camping in the summer. But the first chance he had to trade in his good buddies for a beautiful, blonde-haired, brown-eyed girl from Michigan, he did it in a heartbeat.

God did not create a fraternity brother for Adam. Instead, He gave him a wife. Before there were softball leagues, online sports fantasy teams, and bratwurst with grilled peppers and onions, God knew the deepest need of Adam's heart and gave him Eve to be his life's companion.

> *The LORD God said, It is not good for the man to be alone. I will make*
> *a helper suitable for him.* (Genesis 2:18)

It's such a tragedy when husbands and wives fail to give and receive love by being best friends and enjoying emotional camaraderie. They are missing out on one of the primary reasons God created marriage.

Back to the Basics of Friendship

If the two of you are not best friends, you may have to stop and ask why. Is it because you can't talk without soon arguing? You now focus only on the other person's faults and weaknesses? You have failed to forgive one another and have a storehouse of grievances and resentments? You can't stop stepping on each other's pain?

If the two of you are not best friends,
you may have to stop and ask why.

It may be time to go back to the basics of friendship: unconditional acceptance, shared values, appreciation for the other person's personality, and spending time together just having fun.

Many people can go without sex and still enjoy life but few can be content going through life without a close friend. Virtually every friendless male we have counseled has been lonely, discouraged, and hurting. People don't want spouses with the Companion Heart just so they can have sex. They want such spouses so they can have *meaningful* sex.

The saddest men we know, whether single or married, are those who get their sex from one-night stands, pornography, or prostitutes. While their physical needs may be met, their emotional needs are left as parched as the Sahara Desert. For the Companion Heart, sexual fulfillment does not produce emotional camaraderie. Instead, emotional camaraderie produces sexual fulfillment.

I'm Dreaming of a White Christmas

The final characteristic of the Companion Heart is undying loyalty between a husband and wife. They are faithful and support one another.

One of our favorite Christmastime movies is *White Christmas* with Bing Crosby and Danny Kaye. The romantic musical comedy doesn't have a spell-binding plot, nor is the dialogue particularly crisp or captivating. We usually fast-forward through the seemingly endless choreography sketches.

What makes the story a Christmas classic is its compelling theme of loyalty.

The movie tells the story of two soldiers, portrayed by Bing Crosby and Danny Kaye, who survive World War II, come home and try to make it as entertainers. They travel from city to city, looking for their first big break. Finally, their luck turns when they meet two attractive sisters (Rosemary Clooney and Vera-Ellen) on a train. They end up getting a gig at an expensive nightclub in New York City.

Then they learn that their former commanding general has retired from the Army and purchased a ski resort in Vermont. The only problem is, it hasn't snowed all winter and he's about to go broke if it doesn't snow soon. (This was before artificial snow machines.)

The two friends decide to move their entire nightclub show up to Vermont to put on a benefit performance to save the general. They contact as many old Army buddies as they can find to ask them to come to Vermont—at their own expense at Christmastime—to support their old commanding officer.

The most poignant moment in the movie is when the general comes downstairs and sees nearly 100 men lined up in their Army uniforms standing at ramrod attention. He walks up and down the line, inspecting the troops just as he used to during the war. In typical alpha male fashion, he first derides them for sloppy appearance, poor posture, and overall failures to meet regulations. Then fighting back tears, he tells them that they are the best sight he's ever seen in his life.

Women who watch this timeless holiday classic may be drawn to the two sisters and their romantic misadventures. That's understandable because the Romantic Heart is also one of the main themes of the movie. But men who watch the movie often sum up the story in one word: loyalty.

A Cord of Loyalty Is Not Easily Broken

Loyalty is the willingness to be there for the other person when the chips are down. Recall our earlier story about the husband whose wife suffered from Alzheimer's disease. He gently tied a strip of cloth around his wife's ankle and his own so she would not wander alone in the middle of the night.

The cloth binding them together mirrored the undying loyalty between life-long companions. A man doesn't spend five years caring for a wife who doesn't even remember his name just because they had sex for five decades. He stays with her because they were loyal companions to one another. As the Bible says, *"A friend loves at all times, and a brother is born for adversity"* (Proverbs 17:17).

It's loyalty that produces good sex,
not good sex that produces loyalty.

The Companion Heart gives and receives love through expressions of undying loyalty. When a wife makes loves to her husband after he's laid off, that's loyalty. When a husband makes love to his wife despite her mastectomy to battle cancer, that's loyalty. When a couple patiently works together to overcome prostate surgery or erectile dysfunction due to aging, high blood pressure, depression, or diabetes, that's loyalty. It's loyalty that produces good sex, not good sex that produces loyalty.

A Test of Loyalty

The Companion Heart displays loyalty both inside and outside the bedroom. It can mean standing by spouses when they make the worst mistakes of their lives.

We once heard the testimony of a couple who endured one of the darkest chapters any marriage could pass through. After several years of marriage, the husband sat down with his wife and admitted he had had five affairs, the last one with her best friend. Her life crumbled in just one day. Yet the two of them decided to fight for their marriage and sought out a ministry to heal their hearts. When she prayed out loud to forgive her husband for his betrayal, his tough exterior cracked and he cried like a baby.

It took incredible courage, a supernatural portion of grace, and an eighteen-wheeler filled with loyalty for their marriage to be restored, but restored it was.

In cases of avaricious adultery and ongoing betrayal, a spouse may have no choice but to separate. In this case, however, the husband sincerely repented in genuine brokenness, making reconciliation possible. According to the pastor who worked with them, "They are the now the happiest couple in the city I know. Repentance, brokenness, and loyalty saved the day."

Counterfeit of the Companion Heart

Let's turn our attention to the most common counterfeit of the Companion Heart and how it can ruin a couple's sexual relationship. We'll call it the Conditional Heart. This heart says we'll remain friends, companions, and loyal to one another just as long as it works for both of us. If our feelings change, if times get particularly hard, or you don't give me the same sexual thrills you once did, then it's time for this friendship to end.

The Conditional Heart says we'll remain loyal just as long as it works for both of us.

Perhaps you met when you were both in your twenties. Your bodies looked like you were born at the health club, grew up lifting weights and running marathons, and ate only salads and lean meats, legumes, or nuts. You had muscles or curves in all the right places. During the first year of your marriage, you had sex more than once a day. Maybe you even spent all weekend in bed until you were both exhausted.

Fast forward twenty or thirty years. Your broad minds and narrow waists have swapped places. He thinks, "Boy, having four kids has really wrecked her figure." She thinks, "Is it just me, or does his stomach enter a room before the rest of him?" Sex is now by appointment and requires at least one hour's notice for various prescription drugs to take effect.

The Conditional Heart looks at the spouse and thinks, "This isn't the person I signed up for. I'm not sure I'm as attracted as I used to be. Why should I have to be loyal to someone who hasn't kept up their part of the bargain?"

Unrealistic expectations, extreme self-focus, and the resulting anger now start to undo the threads of friendship woven together in previous years. Add the fear of mortality that starts to creep into mid-life and you often have the formula for a crisis of loyalty. Fearing life is slipping away, someone decides to see if the grass is greener on the other side of the fence before it is too late. That's when the Conditional Heart tragically heads for the door and into the arms of another.

The Companion Heart is vital to a couple's sexual relationship and integrity because it says, "Come what may, regardless of how our bodies may change or even fail us, no matter what sexual experiences we may no longer be able to enjoy, we will remain faithful to each other to the very end."

Handle with Care

So how can we nurture and support the Companion Heart in our spouse?

It is important to remind them over and over again that you believe God brought you together. Tell them you were designed just for each other, that this is a friendship created in heaven before it was made on earth.

This is a friendship created in heaven
before it was made on earth.

Take your wife into your arms, look lovingly into her eyes, and tell her, "You and you alone, out of everyone I ever met or could meet—you alone were meant for me and I was meant for you."

Put your arms around your husband, look deeply into his eyes, and say, "You are the most wonderful husband and friend I could ever have."

Wouldn't that move your romantic needle a few degrees to the right or possibly all the way into the red zone?

What Were the Chances?

Care for your spouse's Companion Heart by sharing your love story with others. It brings assurance that God did indeed make you for each other. At marriage conferences, we ask couples to consider how many things had to go right for the two of them to meet each other. Was it two, three, or maybe even five things lining up just right for them to meet, fall in love, and get married? No, that's not even close.

It takes hundreds of circumstances all working together for you to meet your spouse.

It takes hundreds, if not thousands, of circumstances all working together for you to meet your spouse. You have to be born in the same era, perhaps live in the same state, maybe go to the same school or church, or somehow just run into each other at just the right time. You both had to survive numerous childhood diseases, potentially fatal accidents, and a host of other dangerous situations. Your parents also had to survive such numerous life-threatening moments as did your grandparents and great-grandparents. Do you see our point? It could hardly be fate or karma that you two met.

Bob's father, Homer, nearly died of typhoid fever as an infant. The doctor told Homer's parents to take a photo of him because he wouldn't live another twenty-four hours. Bob's mother, Inez, was born with multiple problems that were so serious, a priest was summoned to baptize her before she died. Amazingly, neither died in infancy and as result, Bob was born decades later. Chance? Karma? Or God working out His divine plan?

We often laugh at how we must have been meant for each other because we were both overachievers in high school. We both appeared on almost every page of our high school yearbooks because we each belonged to so many clubs and organizations. Bob also received two awards the night of his high school senior banquet: "Class Clown" and "Most Likely to Succeed." The first turned out to be prophetic; the second just wishful thinking.

The Best Sex Is with the One Person Meant for You

If you believe God truly meant you for each other, it will make every sexual encounter much more meaningful and satisfying. You are having sex with the one person on earth who God specifically designed to bless and satisfy you. Even if you previously had other sexual partners in life, none can complete you in mind, body, and spirit the way your spouse does.

You can also care for the Companion Heart by guarding your spouse's confidences. Real friends can tell one another their deepest secrets and know no one else will ever learn of them. All of us need someone to whom we can confide our fears, insecurities, and even failures. We know they will treat such information with great care and never divulge to others anything to embarrass, shame, or humiliate us.

*Sexual intimacy is only possible if we
treat each other's secrets as sacred trusts.*

Sexual intimacy is only possible if we treat each other's secrets as sacred trusts. The sexual act by nature exposes who we are with startling clarity and honesty. Modesty should be practiced both before and after marriage because there is certain information about our bodies that only our spouse should know. One popular book for young women by Dannah Gresh is rightly entitled, *Secret Keeper: The Delicate Power of Modesty.*[17] Not even couples who are engaged have a right to each other's physical secrets before marriage. Forfeiting our modesty through defrauding and premarital sex can lead to unintended consequences that damage the relationship.

Even after marriage, caring for the Companion Heart requires you to carefully guard the intimate details of your sexual relationship with your spouse. The secrets of your life of sexual intimacy are not be shared at Starbucks, overheard as you chat on your iPhone, or posted on Twitter, Facebook, reddit, or Snapchat. Doing so wounds the trust and friendship you need to maintain in your marriage.

---

17. Dannah Gresh, *Secret Keeper: The Delicate Power of Modesty* (Chicago, IL: Moody Publishers, 2002)

The Last Full Measure of Devotion

A final way to care for the Companion Heart is to stand up for each other in life. Good friends don't sit back and let others speak ill of their spouses, or mistreat them. They are willing to take on anyone who would do them harm.

Sonny Melton was a registered nurse at a Tennessee hospital. His wife, Heather, was an orthopedic surgeon there. Both were excited about being in Las Vegas to hear country singer Eric Church. They wore T-shirts to celebrate their marriage and the outdoor concert.

Like hundreds of others at that concert, they did not know a deranged gambler named Stephen Paddock was stockpiling an armory of high-powered weapons and ammunition in a high-rise hotel above them. People in the crowd screamed in disbelief and terror as the shooting started and their loved ones fell over beside them.

Once the shooting started, Sonny Melton decided to act.

"He saved my life," Dr. Melton said after the massacre. "He grabbed me from behind (to shield her) and started running when I felt him get shot in the back." Sonny slumped to the ground and died before her eyes. "At this point, I'm in complete disbelief and despair," she said. "Sonny was the most kind-hearted, loving man I have ever met."[18]

By literally laying down his life for his wife, Sonny Melton demonstrated the last full measure of devotion, loyalty, and friendship of the Companion Heart. Their marital friendship was put to the ultimate test and it prevailed. He died protecting his wife.

We may never be called up to make the ultimate sacrifice on behalf of our spouse. But each day, we can demonstrate the depth of our soul-ties, emotional camaraderie, and undying loyalty for one another in big and small ways. As we do, we discover the extraordinary power of true and lasting friendship to immeasurably and positively impact our life of sexual intimacy.

The enduring lesson of the Companion Heart? Good friends make for great sex in the life-long bond of marriage.

---

18. https://nypost.com/2017/10/02/wife-of-las-vegas-massacre-victim-he-saved-my-life-and-lost-his

Questions to Consider:

1. Why is it important to understand God created the Companion Heart before sin entered the world?

_____

_____

_____

_____

_____

2. How many things had to go just right for you and your spouse to meet, fall in love, and get married?

_____

_____

_____

_____

_____

3. How can knowing you were meant for each other strengthen your life of sexual intimacy?

_____

_____

_____

_____

_____

God's Word to Consider:

"A man of many companions may come to ruin, but there is a friend who sticks closer than a brother." (Proverbs 18:24)

_____

_____

_____

_____

_____

_____

_____

_____

_____

_____

_____

_____

_____

_____

_____

_____

_____

_____

_____

5

THE GIVING HEART

The husband should fulfill his marital duty to his wife,
nd likewise the wife to her husband. The wife does not have authority
over her own body but yields it to her husband.
In the same way, the husband does not have authority over his own
body but yields it to his wife.
Do not deprive each other except perhaps by mutual consent and for a
time, so that you may devote yourselves to prayer.
Then come together again so that Satan will not tempt you
because of your lack of self-control.
—1 Corinthians 7:3–5

The Giving Heart gives and receives love by joyfully providing for their spouse's sexual needs and offering themselves in loving surrender.

> *If it's true giving is better than receiving,*
> *then offer sex freely, frequently, and generously.*

The first time Bob asked Cheryl out on a date was at 6:15 a.m. on a Saturday. We were both single and in seminary; Cheryl had a part-time job on campus. Bob learned through a mutual friend that Cheryl and her current boyfriend were going to break up Friday night at 5:30 p.m. This informant/friend also told him Cheryl started her Saturday morning job, answering phones in the administration building, at 6:00 a.m.

Now some may be thinking, "Bob knew when Cheryl started work? Stalker!"

Bob says, "No, I was not stalking her. ... Okay, maybe I was."

At precisely 6:01 a.m. on Saturday morning, Bob strolled through the ornate reception area—complete with Greek revival arches over the doorway, vaulted beige ceilings, and life-size color murals of heroes of the faith—trying to act nonchalant.

Cheryl was reading a book when Bob went over to her desk. "Hey, what's up?" he said. Cheryl looked up, then looked around, somewhat astonished that anyone would be in the reception area this early in the morning. For the next several minutes, Bob did his best to be witty and engaging. Cheryl kept wondering, *What's he want?*

After about fifteen minutes, Bob finally said, "How would you like to go out this evening? I'd like to take you to some place nice."

Cheryl hesitated for a moment, then smiled with those big brown eyes and said sweetly, "Okay."

Bob tried not to act surprised. "Great. I'll pick you up at five." Trying harder than he should have to be suave and casual, he raised his right eyebrow. "We're going to a nice restaurant so you might want to dress up."

Cheryl did dress up—in fact, she looked stunning. And as Bob pulled up in front of her dormitory in his father's humongous Oldsmobile 88 sedan, she was a little impressed. Homer's car was built in the era of "gun boats," big and long.

We drove forty-five minutes away to a restaurant listed on the National Register of Historic Places. For two seminary students on their first date, it was quite elegant—perhaps a little too elegant. The tables were resplendent with fine china, crystal glassware, shining silver flatware, pewter pitchers, and spotless linen tablecloths.

As the maître d' seated us and handed out menus, Bob looked across the table and said, "Order whatever you like." His intention was to convey the dubiously accurate message, "Money is no object."

Cheryl did order whatever she liked. When the bill came and the waiter handed it to Bob, he looked at it and gulped. Not wishing to appear nonplussed, he casually reached for his wallet in his coat pocket.

Nothing there. He then reached into the other inside coat pocket. Nothing again. He reached into a pants pocket. Empty.

All Bob's wriggling and squirming caught Cheryl's attention. "Is anything wrong?"

"Did you bring any money with you?"

"What?" Cheryl's face turned pink. "Why?"

"My wallet," Bob gulped. "I forgot my wallet."

You never get a second chance to make a first impression. In Cheryl's eyes, Bob just blew it.

Praying that the waiter would take his time to return to their table, Bob looked at Cheryl with imploring eyes. Sensing the gravity of the situation, Cheryl opened her wallet and pulled out two crumpled one dollar bills. Bob looked at the forlorn pictures of George Washington. "Do they have any friends?"

Cheryl proceeded to dig furiously through her purse. "Maybe you could just dump it out," Bob said. Cheryl pursed her lips, turned her brown purse over, and shook out its contents. Among the eyeliner, lipstick, and other items that fell out on to the table were several coins. We began to tally up what we had.

After two or three minutes of discussion about the possibility of washing dishes to pay the bill, Bob calmly produced his wallet and held it up for Cheryl to see. "I was only kidding," he said with a grin.

For the record, Cheryl thought the whole incident was funny—eventually.

While Bob's sense of humor might have been somewhat misguided, by taking Cheryl to the finest restaurant he knew and buying the best meal for her that he could afford, he was trying to convey an important message: *whatever I have that would bring you joy, I want to give it to you.* Through the years, she has sent back the same message in countless ways.

That is the essence of the Giving Heart.

Did God Intend Sex to Be a Gift or a Weapon?

The anguished voice on the phone conveyed the deep hurt, confusion, and sense of rejection the husband was feeling. "It's been almost a year since we've made love," he said forlornly. "She actually told me I should go find someone else if I need sex because I won't be getting it for her."

Contrast this with the woman who had some sage premarital advice for her soon-to-be-married younger sister. "Always try to say yes to your husband. It's such a simple gesture of love you can offer." She grinned at the bride-to-be. "And it makes him sooo happy."

The question in many marriages comes down this: should sex be used as a tool to get what I want or as a gift offered in unselfish love?

*Should sex be used as a tool to get what I want
or as a gift offered in unselfish love?*

While the popular myth is that wives sometimes use sex as a bargaining tool, we've seen husbands who do the same thing. A heartbroken wife told us she felt rejected and unwanted because her husband had not made love to her even once in the last year. Instead, he had actually moved into a different room and told her never to cross the doorway.

Some spouses, realizing their mates have an unrelenting need for sexual fulfillment, discover the power of withholding sex from them. They make it a weapon of choice in the battle to gain control of the marriage.

An author we mentioned previously, Willard Harley[14], a nationally acclaimed licensed clinical psychologist and marriage counselor, speculates that sexual fulfillment is the number one emotional need of men in marriage. If this is true, then withholding sex from a husband strikes at his emotional core. It can leave lasting heart damage if regularly employed as a bargaining tool or instrument of manipulation.

Let's look at the primary characteristics of the Giving Heart as it plays out in a married couple's life of sexual intimacy.

First, the Giving Heart gives and receives love by an unselfish and eager desire to provide for the spouse's sexual needs.

The goal of the Giving Heart is to bring your spouse deep joy and lasting fulfillment by providing them with sex on a regular basis. The need for regular sexual fulfillment is well-documented, even in ancient history.

Legend has it that the costly and brutal war between the Greeks and the Trojans finally came to an end when wives on both sides made a pact not to give their husbands sex until they stopped their senseless fighting.

Apparently, both armies decided they were more interested in making love than war. When faced with a choice between the battlefield and the bedroom, the men voted with their feet and went home.

More than Just Reporting for Duty

*Both husbands and wives are to
make themselves available to their spouses to fulfill
their sexual needs on a regular basis.*

The Scriptures are quite clear that both husbands and wives are to make themselves available to their spouses to fulfill their sexual needs on a regular basis. This is an essential part of our commitment to the marriage covenant. Paul writes, *"The husband should fulfill his marital duty to his wife, and likewise the wife to her husband"* (1 Corinthians 7:3).

While the Bible uses the word "duty" to describe the mutual obligation to fulfill one another's sexual needs, the word "duty" in the original language refers to "that which is owed," "a marital responsibility," or even a "debt."

When we marry, we enter into something of a moral contract. We agree to a mutual understanding that we will be the exclusive and sole provider of sexual intimacy and fulfillment for a spouse. Furthermore, it won't be just when we feel like it or are finally in the mood. Rather, we will provide loving and willing access to sex on a regular and sustained basis. Implicit in this agreement is the promise we will never seek sexual fulfillment from anyone or anything else because that would constitute adultery.

We are left only with each other as the sole provider of sexual satisfaction and intimacy.

The result of this moral, spiritual, and legal contract of marriage is that we are left only with each other as the sole provider of sexual satisfaction and intimacy. This life-long, God-designed monopoly makes our spouse the only person on earth who can supply us with sex on a regular basis.

When one spouse withholds sex for purely selfish purposes, you could argue it constitutes a breach of contract. Given that marriages create a relational monopoly of sorts, if you begin to change the terms of the agreement simply to get your own way, you are being dishonest, unfair, and manipulative. You pledged on your wedding day you wouldn't do that.

We have seen many marriages nearly fall apart or dissolve in divorce because one spouse or the other decided to withhold sex for months simply because they could. One woman refused to have sex with her husband until he bought her a new car. The pain, anger, and frustration resulting from her unilateral embargo on sex virtually destroyed what little love remained in their marriage.

Men Misusing Scripture

At the same time, there are few portions of the New Testament that uncaring and self-focused husbands abuse more often than 1 Corinthians 7:3–4: *"The husband should fulfill his marital duty to his wife, and likewise the wife to her husband. The wife does not have authority over her own body but yields it to her husband. In the same way, the husband does not have authority over his own body but yields it to his wife."*

Although they could be insensitive, domineering, and even abusive in their behavior when their wives draw back from providing them with sex, they will yank this passage out of context and use it as a spiritual club: "You can't say no to me. The Bible says you are supposed to give me sex whenever I want it." They ignore the fact that although Paul first says the wife should yield to her husband, he then notes the husband should yield to his wife as well. They also ignore the larger context of Scripture that commands husbands to treat their wives with sacrificial love, tender respect, and equal value.

Secular people who don't know the Bible can do the same thing. Sadly, some take it to the extreme, using physical intimidation to get the sex they want, when they want it. A music video from the 1990s featured a woman with a black eye, a wounded heart, and tears running down her cheeks, all given to her by a cruel and violent husband. He would beat her and then afterwards demand sex.

One day, she had finally suffered enough. In a final act of desperate revenge after they had "made love" and he was sound asleep, she set the house on fire. The theme of the tragic video was her "Independence Day."[19] While murdering her husband was the morally wrong way to escape such ongoing mental, physical, and sexual abuse, he had also abused his "rights" to an extreme measure—one that God never intended.

Scripture is never to be used as an ultimatum to manipulate a spouse into submission.

God's Word presents the Giving Heart in the context of a loving, caring, and sensitive marriage. This portion of Scripture is never to be used as an ultimatum to manipulate a spouse into submission. Scripture knows

---

19. Martina McBride, "Independence Day," on *The Way That I Am* (RCA Records, 1993)

nothing of the selfish attitude, "It doesn't matter how I treat you. You owe me because that's what the Bible says."

It Is Truly More Blessed to Give than Receive

Rather, the Giving Heart goes far beyond a mere sense of duty or obligation. It sees the enormous potential for conveying love, honor, and respect, particularly in saying yes with a willing and eager heart to our spouse's request for sexual intimacy. While Jesus said, "It is more blessed to give than to receive" in the context of a cheerful financial contribution to God's Kingdom, there are remarkable similarities to married sexual intimacy—indeed to all of life.

When we give our money, time, and talents in the proper spirit, great reward always comes back to us. Consider how this passage might also be applied to our life of sexual intimacy within the holy covenant of marriage:

> *Give, and it will be given to you. A good measure, pressed down, shaken together and running over, will be poured into your life. For with the measure you use, it will be measured to you.* (Luke 6:38)

The law of sowing and reaping can also be applied to a married couple's life of physical intimacy:

> *Remember this: Whoever sows sparingly will also reap sparingly, and whoever sows generously will also reap generously. Each of you should give what you have decided in your heart to give, not reluctantly or under compulsion, for God loves a cheerful giver.* (2 Corinthians 9:6–7)

Which brings us to the primary passage we need to take to heart in understanding the Giving Heart:

> *Remembering the words the Lord Jesus himself said, It is more blessed to give than to receive.* (Acts 20:35)

The Scriptures teach us that true biblical giving is characterized by abundance, generosity, cheerfulness, and the attitude that blessing another is a privilege. Anyone who provides for their spouse's sexual needs with the proper spirit of the Giving Heart will receive spiritual, emotional, and physical blessings.

True biblical giving is characterized by abundance, generosity, cheerfulness, and the attitude that blessing another is a privilege.

The Wonderful God Who Provides

One of the marvelous Names for God in the Old Testament is Jehovah Jireh, which means "the Lord who provides." It is in the very nature of our Heavenly Father to lovingly provide for all of our needs. Because we are made in the image of God as male and female, we can find joy and fulfillment in providing for our spouse in our lives of intimacy as well as other areas.

God desires a spirit of sacrificial giving in a couple's sexual relationship.

Bob says he is filled with deep gratitude and appreciation for Cheryl, who has so unselfishly strived to meet his sexual needs throughout their marriage. "From the day we married until today, Bob says, "she responded unselfishly to me whenever she could. Even when she was tired or worn out from a long day with the kids or even feeling somewhat ill. She responded to me when we traveled and when we were at home. She seemed eager to continue our sexual relationship as long as possible when we were expecting a child. She would resume intimacy with me just as quickly as prudent after each one of our children was born. She continued blessing me through job losses, housing relocations, and even periods of time when I went through depression. I am among the most blessed of all men I know."

It's a blessing to live with a spouse with the Giving Heart.

There Are Times to Say No

Normally, we would save the following discussion for the Counterfeit Heart section of this chapter. However, because there's a potential for misunderstanding regarding the Giving Heart willingly providing for the spouse's sexual needs on a frequent and regular basis, we offer the following caveat and caution.

The biblical spirit of the Giving Heart does not demand that a husband or wife give in to their spouse's every sexual demand regardless of the time, place, or the other person's current behavior. This is particularly true when pornography or other forms of sexual perversion are sought.

You cannot ask your spouse to sacrifice their sense of dignity, decency, and value.

For spouses to demand that their mates re-enact whatever sexual act they may have viewed recently—online, in an R-rated movie, or a magazine—is not what the sacrificial provision is all about. You cannot ask your spouse to sacrifice their sense of dignity, decency, and value for the sake of fulfilling some sick or twisted obsession. The Bible will have no part of that abuse of the Giving Heart.

One day, while listening to our local Christian radio station, we heard a desperate call from a woman who was clearly distraught—her voice was trembling. Just that morning, as she got out of the shower, her husband demanded that she let him photograph her in degrading poses. She wondered if it was her duty as a wife to participate in such perverted behavior. The answer is clearly no.

The man who wanted his wife to join him in his twisted sexual fantasies would do well to remember this warning:

"I have the right to do anything," you say—but not everything is beneficial....Flee from sexual immorality. All other sins a person commits are outside the body, but whoever sins sexually, sins against their own body. Do you not know that your bodies are temples of the Holy Spirit, who is in you, whom you have received from God? You are not your own.
(1 Corinthians 6:12, 18–19)

Those who view pornography and allow it to inflame their minds with degrading images and unnatural thoughts have no right to ask their spouses to go along with it. Those who demand perverse sexual behavior from their spouses would do well to remember another serious warning from Paul:

> Furthermore, just as they did not think it worthwhile to retain the knowledge of God, so God gave them over to a depraved mind, so that they do what ought not to be done. They have become filled with every kind of wickedness, evil, greed and depravity....Although they know God's righteous decree that those who do such things deserve death, they not only continue to do these very things but also approve of those who practice them.   (Romans 1:28–29, 32)

Not Everything Is Okay Just Because You're Married

To finish this discussion of a misapplication of the Giving Heart, let us address one of the more popular cultural myths held even among some Christians. It appears to push the boundaries as far as possible in terms of what is acceptable sexual behavior:

"As long as we're married, whatever we do is okay."

Can you see the obvious fallacy in this idea? Simply because you have the opportunity to perform a certain sexual act now that you're married doesn't necessarily make it healthy, good, or morally right.

A soldier is given the opportunity to carry an automatic rifle in the service of his country, but he doesn't have the right to shoot anyone he pleases. A teacher needs to maintain discipline in her classroom, but she doesn't have the right to punch a student. A pastor has the opportunity to tell stories from people's lives to illustrate his sermon, but he doesn't have permission to betray the confidences of parishioners.

Yes, the status of marriage allows you to enjoy regular sexual intimacy and a wide range of loving behaviors. You can do these acts without shame, guilt, or condemnation because God has declared the marriage bed to be pure and holy.

However, simply because we're married and have an opportunity to do whatever we please doesn't mean we can or should do something that's unnatural, degrading, or humiliating. The Bible is abundantly clear that the liberty we enjoy as Christians should never be used as a pretext for sin, much less to demand that our spouses join us in our wrongdoing. The Scriptures warn that God will one day judge such behavior: "*The acts of the flesh are obvious: sexual immorality, impurity, and debauchery....I warn you, as I did before, that those who live like this will not inherit the kingdom of God*" (Galatians 5:19, 21).

Now that we've examined some of the misconceptions and misapplications of the Giving Heart, let's turn our attention to all of the promise, joy, and satisfaction it brings when practiced as God intended.

The second characteristic of the Giving Heart is *offering ourselves to one another in joyful trust and surrender*.

The Bible says, "*Do not deprive each other except perhaps by mutual consent, and for a time...*" (1 Corinthians 7:5).

The Bible commands us not to selfishly withhold sex from our spouse. Instead, we are to offer our spouse our loving trust and surrender.

What if one of you simply doesn't have as strong a sex drive as the other? Rather than simply telling your spouse, "That's the way it is. Take it or leave it," God's Word has another suggestion. Practice what some call the "loving surrender" of your heart, mind, and body to your spouse for the sake of unselfishly fulfilling their God-given and legitimate sexual needs.

Years ago, we helped an older couple move from their home of thirty years to a retirement village. Among their boxes of books, we found one written decades ago with the intriguing title, *The Power of Sexual Surrender*. It was written in 1959 by Dr. Marie Robinson, a Cornell-educated psychiatrist.

Amazon.com says the author "devoted her New York City practice to the treatment of frigidity and this book is a result of her work with hundreds of women seeking better sex lives and happier relationships. Although some 'feminists' may consider some of her ideas out-of-favor, her view of the basic nature of men and women remains timeless and of value today in promoting healthy, sane marriages....One reviewer called the book 'the sanest work on feminine psychology ever written.'"[20]

Dr. Robinson's basic thesis seems consistent with Paul's advice in his first letter to the Corinthians. We are to lovingly surrender ourselves to our spouses in trust, vulnerability, and love so we can discover a new and powerful source of fulfillment in our lives. Not a power to manipulate or control another individual, but a power freeing us to enjoy sex with our spouse in trusting abandonment.

Trust is perhaps the key component in loving surrender. Trust is essential to all meaningful relationships. Few things in life demand greater trust than surrendering your body to your spouse in the act of sexual intimacy. Never are our hearts, emotions, dignity, self-worth, value, and personhood as entirely vulnerable as in the act of making love. Nothing about you is hidden from the other person. Your total personhood is involved as you offer your heart to the other person in an atmosphere of radical exposure and honesty. True sexual surrender is impossible without trust.

True sexual surrender is impossible without trust.

When Jesus surrendered His body upon the cross, it was a total and complete surrender of Himself for the sake of love. He had a heart filled with trust in His Heavenly Father, so He could offer His body in loving sacrifice for us and our sins.

When we surrender ourselves to our spouses with hearts full of trust and love, the passion fires burn bright.

The Gift that May Have Saved Bob's Life

Cheryl says, "While I was in college, my boss at a mission organization gave me a hand-carved letter opener as a gift. He had been on a trip to visit missionaries in Africa and brought a gift home for each employee.

20. https://www.amazon.com/Power-Sexual-Surrender-Marie-Robinson/dp/0451069218

"One morning six years later, Bob decided to take the letter opener to the office. After all, our very active little son, R.J., did not need to get his hands on something so sharp. We lived only three houses away from our church in the second highest crime precinct in Minneapolis, but Bob had to drive in that morning to make it to an appointment later.

"Bob pulled up behind our church, opening his car door to get out. At the last moment, he remembered the long, knife-like letter opener, so he reached in and grabbed it off the front seat with his right hand. As he stood up and closed the car door, he sensed someone right behind him. Still holding the opener, Bob turned around to see who it was.

"A young man stood there, with a stocking cap covering most of his face. The moment he saw Bob's knife-like letter opener, he turned around and ran in the other direction.

"Did a gift from Africa, given to me six years earlier, save Bob's life? This much is sure: there's a would-be robber out there who may be wondering what kind of pastor carries a knife to church. I am thankful to God for His hand of protection, so I recount to others the times when God has rescued us."

The third characteristic of the Giving Heart is abstaining from regular sexual relations only by mutual agreement and only for a short period of time.

The apostle Paul recognized there are unusual circumstances that require a married couple to set aside their regular life of sexual intimacy. He said we should use such times for focused prayer, then "come together again" so the devil does not lead us astray.

What does this exception clause to the Giving Heart look like in everyday terms for a married couple? They may forgo sexual intimacy for varying periods of time due to illness, business travel, or childbirth, for example. But there is another legitimate reason to abstain from sex as the apostle Paul suggests—to focus exclusively on prayer and fasting.

Several times in the Old Testament, married couples voluntarily abstained from sexual relations due to the immediate spiritual challenge at hand. For example, as the people of Israel were about to receive the Ten Commandments at Mt. Sinai, they were given specific instructions.

After Moses had gone down the mountain to the people, he consecrated them, and they washed their clothes. Then he said to the people, "Prepare yourselves for the third day. Abstain from sexual relations."

(Exodus 19:14–15)

The people were to devote themselves for a limited time to spiritual introspection and consecration to God. Sexual relations between married couples were not forbidden in general in the camp at Mt. Sinai, but for a short season, they were to set aside their normal passions in order to gain a special and heightened spiritual focus.

Uriah, one of King David's most loyal military officers, gives us another example of voluntarily giving up sex for a season. In this sad story, while Uriah is off fighting, David has an affair with Uriah's wife, Bathsheba, and she becomes pregnant with David's child. To try to cover this up, David tries to persuade Uriah to go home and enjoy making love to his wife for an evening.

David was told, "Uriah did not go home." So he asked Uriah, "Haven't you just come from a military campaign? Why didn't you go home?" Uriah said to David, "The ark and Israel and Judah are staying in tents, and my commander Joab and my lord's men are camped in the open country. How could I go to my house to eat and drink and make love to my wife? As surely as you live, I will not do such a thing!"

(2 Samuel 11:10–11)

In this case, Uriah abstained not because having sex with his wife would have been wrong or disloyal to David, but because it seemed selfish while his comrades were daily facing life and death circumstances on the open battlefield. Uriah's voluntary self-denial was to focus on a higher cause that was ultimately meant to serve and honor the God of Israel.

Don't Give Satan a Foothold

By the time of the New Testament era, early Christians occasionally fasted from fulfilling common human appetites such as eating, drinking, or enjoying sexual relations. Yet it was always to be by mutual agreement and only for a limited time. To ignore these sensible parameters, as the apostle Paul noted, was to invite temptation by the enemy of our souls.

The message of the Bible is clear. To fail to practice the Giving Heart in our married sexual relationship is to open ourselves to Satan's temptations and schemes.

How does this work?

When we unilaterally withhold intimacy from our spouses for unnecessary or selfish reasons, it will eventually wound their hearts. The pain can cause them to become angry or bitter, which can culminate in an impulsive choice to find sexual release somewhere else.

Do we really want to make our beloved suffer by deliberately withholding sexual intimacy in marriage? Can you imagine how Satan might be rubbing his hands with glee in anticipation of the destructive choices they might make? According to Paul, unresolved anger alone gives the devil a foothold in our lives. (See Ephesians 4:26–27.)

When we deny our spouse their legitimate access to sexual intimacy, it inevitably wounds their heart.

When we deny our spouse their legitimate access to sexual intimacy, it inevitably wounds their heart. The theologian and author Marcus Warner observes that emotional wounds give the devil an opportunity to introduce lies into our minds. These lies include such things as, "She doesn't love you," "Your husband hates you," "There's no point in trying in this marriage any longer," or "You're a failure as a spouse."

Jesus warned that our enemy is a liar and when he lies to us, he is speaking his native language. Do you or I want to be responsible for giving Satan the wide-open opportunity to plant negative, deceptive, and soul-destroying thoughts in our spouse's heart, all because we decided to start withholding sexual intimacy?

Breaking a Solemn Vow

Withholding sexual intimacy without a legitimate biblical reason to do so is to practice a form of emotional blackmail or deception. Again, we might even call it a breach of contract. Remember what you promised (vowed) to your spouse on your wedding day?

The wedding vows we exchanged on June 16, 1979, in front of friends, witnesses, and God Himself, included these words:

> "I, Bob/Cheryl, take thee to be my wife/husband, to have and to hold, from this day forward, for better, for worse, for richer, for poorer, in sickness and in health, to love and to cherish, till death do us part, and thereto I pledge thee my faith." We then exchanged rings and said, "In token and pledge of constant love and abiding faith, with this ring, I thee wed; in the name of the Father and of the Son and of the Holy Spirit. Amen."

When we promise to love, honor, and cherish our mates, and to keep ourselves for them alone as long as we live, everyone knows what we are talking about. We are promising not only sexual fidelity, but sexual availability.

It's sad when a married spouse, apart from serious reasons such as infidelity or physical abuse, decides to play the ultimate trump card and deny the other sexual fulfillment. Be honest. Do you think your spouse would really have married you knowing you were going to play that game for days, weeks, months, or even years on end? No, our spouses believe us when we promise to love and cherish them. Withholding sex to make a point or leverage the relationship is neither loving nor cherishing—it is manipulative, destructive behavior based on a breach of vows.

Withholding sex to make a point or leverage the relationship is manipulative, destructive behavior.

Jesus taught us in the Lord's Prayer to pray to our Father, "Lead us not into temptation but deliver us from evil." When we shut our spouse out of the bedroom either literally or figuratively, we may very well be leading them into temptation. Do you want to be responsible for that?

When we have the Giving Heart, we regularly and frequently engage in mutual, fulfilling sexual intimacy in marriage. It's keeping our promise—no more, no less.

Counterfeits of the Giving Heart

We spoke earlier in this chapter about the Withholding Heart. There are other common counterfeits or distortions of the Giving Heart that can take place in marriage.

1. The Obligated Heart

Spouses with the Obligated Heart acknowledge Scripture enjoins them to provide their mates with regular sexual intimacy, but rather than rejoicing in this command, they chafe at it. They see providing sex as nothing more than an unwelcome duty or irritating obligation. They may go through with the act, but their heart is not in it. And their mate knows it.

The Obligated Heart sees sex as an unwelcome duty or irritating obligation.

Or the Obligated Heart may pretend to be enjoying the sexual encounter, but cannot wait for it to be over. They never hesitate to find any and every excuse to put it off for another time. It doesn't take long for the spouse to catch on. Their husband or wife really wishes they didn't have to do this. Such reluctance strikes at the heart of the other's self-respect, enjoyment, and sense of value.

All of us have been through experiences in which someone pretended to be interested in spending time with us but were clearly looking for the exit signs.

One of Bob's earliest experiences in dating was to invite a girl to an all-day track meet at his school. The girl agreed to go with him in a group setting and almost from the crack of the starting pistol, she found another boy she was more interested in. For the rest of that tortuously long day, this girl and the other guy laughed, joked, and walked together. Meanwhile, Bob continued to shell out money for her at the concession stand, for the school raffle, and for other vendors who walked by. He ended up feeling like Chump for a Day (with no change left either) as he personally financed this girl and her love interest's first date.

The Obligated Heart doesn't fool a husband or wife for very long. If you find your spouse's requests for sexual intimacy irritating and more a duty than a delight, they will eventually get the message. The Obligated Heart usually doesn't realize all of the lasting damage it's doing to the relationship. They are dynamiting their marriage. They hope that if they just keep rolling their eyes, taking a deep breath, and saying, "Okay, I guess," or appearing bored and disinterested during the act of intimacy, the day will come when their mates will quit asking. Perhaps they will—as they pack their bags and walk out the door.

If you are successful in finally destroying your spouse's interest in having sex with you, it's no victory to celebrate. The only thing you will have accomplished is dropping a wrecking ball from ten stories high onto their heart. Sex was never designed or intended by God to be a chore, burden, or nuisance. To act as if it is would be extremely hurtful to your spouse.

2. The Bargaining Heart

While the Obligated Heart looks at sex as nothing more than an irritating chore, like scrubbing the shower floor, the Bargaining Heart sees it a little differently. Here is a golden opportunity to exert some serious leverage and pressure to get their spouse to do something.

The Bargaining Heart sees sex as a golden opportunity to exert some leverage.

"You want to make love? Okay, I need you to first to apologize for not spending more time with my family on the Fourth of July." Not every marriage descends into such blatant arm-twisting. It can take far more subtle forms. "Sure, we can go away for the weekend. But first, did you paint the family room? I've been asking you to do that for six months."

Sex was never meant to be a bargaining tool. You are not management and your spouse is not the union. To use what God designed to be a sacred and selfless gift as a manipulative, maneuvering, and clever bargaining chip is morally wrong.

Bargaining Hearts know their spouses need sex—and perhaps are even desperate for it. Instead of joyfully providing for their needs in the spirit of the Giving Heart, they cynically negotiate a deal, one that actually comes quite close to the spirit of prostitution. "I'll give you sex if you first pay up..." It's a lot like the deals made in Times Square on a Friday evening, even if the payment is as simple as agreeing to host the neighborhood cookout or buy a new couch.

3. The Complaining Heart

The final counterfeit or distortion for the Giving Heart is the Complaining Heart. It can rob the joy or fulfillment from sexual intimacy like nothing else. Complaining can range from subtle put-downs regarding your performance as a lover to protests that you are over-sexed and need professional help. A spouse with a Complaining Heart may say, "That's it? But I'm not satisfied," or "Can't you find anything sexier to wear than that old nightie?," or "That was sure same old, same old..."

The Complaining Heart may voice subtle put-downs regarding the spouse's sexual performance.

Take any joyful and anticipated day, start it with complaints and pretty soon, the entire atmosphere of the event will be ruined. One of our relatives came from a complaining family. They could turn a day at Disneyland into a remake of *Escape from Alcatraz*. On a short road trip, the driver decided he'd try to put a stop to the chronic complaining. Before they left the drive-way, he turned around and said, "Let's make an agreement. If I catch any of you complaining during the trip, I will fine you a nickel." We don't know for sure, but we suspect he returned with a pocketful of change.

The Giving Heart knows that complaining kills joy, anticipation, and fulfillment in sexual intimacy. Therefore, look for reasons to bless your spouse and frequently compliment him or her on sexual appeal and per-formance. Sex in marriage is a work in progress, not a score card. Find something positive to say, regardless of how disappointing your lovemak-ing might be from time to time. Bob once heard this sage advice from an elderly educator: "Even when sex is bad, it is still very good." He was on to something.

Sex in marriage is a work in progress, not a score card.

Give Thanks Between the Sheets

An attitude of entitlement seems to have taken over, even among many Christians. Some people seem to think, "Why should I thank you? You owe it to me." Yet few things can deflate your joy when giving more than someone who ignores your generosity or complains about the gift.

On one occasion, Bob offered his stocking cap to a homeless man shiv-ering on a train platform during a freezing January day in Chicago. The man wore a plastic grocery bag on his head in an effort to keep warm. Bob had an internal struggle about offering his cap to the freezing man. He had purchased it at an Army surplus store while shopping there with our son, who was serving in the military at the time. It was a symbol of the bond between them and the pride Bob felt in our son for serving our country.

But the homeless man was clearly in danger of frostbite or hypother-mia. Bob wrestled with God for a moment before he slowly removed the cap from his head and offered it to the homeless man. "Would you like this?" he asked him.

"Only if it fits me," the homeless man replied, showing no emotion. He put it on his head and it did fit. "Okay, I'll guess I'll keep it," he said—and walked away without even a mumbled word of thanks. He could not have known of Bob's emotional sacrifice in parting with the cap.

Regularly Thank Your Spouse for Providing for Your Sexual Needs

When it comes to expressing thanks to our spouse with the Giving Heart, we need to be specific and genuine. "I am such a blessed man (or woman) to have someone so giving like you," or "Thank you for giving me the gift of your love and meeting my sexual needs in such an amazing way," or "How did I ever deserve a wife (or husband) who never says no to my requests for sex? I am one of the most fortunate people on earth."

Look for ways to express the Giving Heart in other areas of your marriage besides the bedroom. Rarely do spouses give in order to receive. It's usually the farthest thing on the mind of someone who knows the true joy of giving just to give.

We once heard a podcast of Pastor Jim Cymbala recounting the early days of his ministry at the Brooklyn Tabernacle Church in New York. He started with virtually no guaranteed salary. His family lived in a house they bought with money borrowed from his in-laws. One day, he opened the refrigerator and found nothing inside. "Whoa," he said, "I guess it's time we get some groceries."

The problem was, he had no money. As Jim stood staring into the chilly abyss of his empty refrigerator, the doorbell rang. Not expecting guests, he went to the door to see who it was. He stepped outside in time to see a car speed away down the block. And stacked on his front porch were six bags of groceries. To this day, Jim doesn't know who left the food for him and his family. The person with the Giving Heart didn't need for him to know.

Spouses with the Giving Heart do not give in order to get, but we still need to thank them. Perhaps taking on a common household task in order to give your beloved some much needed free time. Or giving your spouse a foot massage at the end of a particularly long day when he or she has been standing for hours. Or buying a thank-you card on the way home from work and listing all the reasons you thank God for your spouse. You can never say thank-you too often.

Go Public with Your Praise

One final way to care for spouses with the Giving Heart is praise them in front of others.

Obviously, you should not go into the details about how and why you are so fortunate to have a spouse who willingly and regularly provides you with sex. Nonetheless, you should express your love, admiration, and gratitude for your spouse for having a giving character and heart. Praise them till they blush when the two of you are present in front of family, friends, and coworkers. It will mean the world to them.

Praise your spouse in front of family, friends, and coworkers.

Unfortunately, so much humor is about the tensions we cause each other in marriage rather than the joys we offer to one another. When you hear other men or women complaining about their spouses, even reference their poor sexual performance, it's time to speak up.

"I can't relate to what you are saying," you can tell them. "I have been blessed with one of the most unselfish, giving, and wonderful people anyone could ever have. There isn't a day I don't thank God for him (or her)." The spouse roast will come to a quick end.

No Greater Love

During a dark winter night on January 23, 1943, the U.S. Army Transport Dorchester quietly left New York Harbor. The converted civilian cruise ship carried some 900 American soldiers. Its first destination was Greenland; from there, it was to travel to a foreign destination known only to the captain and his immediate officers.

Three Coast Guard vessels accompanied the lightly armed troop transport ship. Somewhere off the coast of Newfoundland, Canada, the Coast

Guard detected the possible presence of a dreaded German U-boat subma-rine. Dorchester's captain ordered all of the soldiers on board to don their life jackets just in case they came under attack. But most of the men chose to ignore the order because they were already sweltering and the jackets were uncomfortable.

After midnight on the morning of February 3, 1943, an eerie peri-scope surfaced above the water. The captain of the enemy submarine put the Dorchester in its deadly crosshairs. Like hungry metal sharks released from a cage, the torpedoes dashed full speed toward the lower hull of the troop ship. They hit their target dead-on and several explosions rocked the Dorchester. The ship lost electricity. Suddenly, nearly a thousand men were groping in the pitch dark to get to the upper deck.

On board the ill-fated ship were four U.S. Army chaplains, all from distinctly different religious backgrounds.[21] They were: George Fox, a Methodist; Alexander Goode, a Reform Jewish rabbi; Clark Poling, a Reformed Church pastor; and Father John Washington, a Catholic priest. Each had been stationed on the ship following their training at Harvard University.

After the German attack, the four clergymen, sensing the gravity of the situation, quickly went into action. Standing atop the stairs leading from lower deck to the main deck, they methodically handed out life jack-ets to each terrified soldier as he appeared from below. The supply of life jackets soon ran out and scores of men were still scrambling upwards. One by one, each of the chaplains took off his own life jacket and handed it to the next panicked soldier headed for a lifeboat.

The water in the Atlantic was just thirty-four degrees Fahrenheit. One of the soldiers swimming away from the sinking ship witnessed a remark-able scene on deck. "As I swam away from the ship, I looked back," he said. "The flares had lighted everything. The bow came up high and she slid un-der. The last thing I saw, the four chaplains were up there praying for the safety of the men. They had done everything they could. I did not see them again. They themselves did not have a chance without their life jackets."[22]

---

21. http://www.fourchaplains.org
22. https://en.wikipedia.org/wiki/Four_Chaplains

As the ship slipped into its watery grave, prayers could be heard—offered in English, Hebrew, and Latin—coming from the main deck of the ship. Those four chaplains perished, along nearly 670 of the 904 men on board.

Their story of willing sacrifice has not been forgotten. It has been memorialized in movies, documentaries, books, and even musical compositions. They are remembered to this day for their Giving Hearts.

Whenever we truly give of ourselves solely for the benefit and well-being of another, we come as close to the character of the Divine as may be possible in this life. Jesus said, *"Greater love has no one than this: to lay down one's life for one's friends"* (John 15:13). The Dorchester's chaplains are often called "the Four Immortal Chaplains" because the impact of their selfless sacrifice lives on forever.

While each of the Six Hearts of Intimacy reflect the heart of God in some unique way, perhaps none is closer to our loving Heavenly Father's heart than the Giving Heart. *"For God so loved the world that he gave his one, and only Son, that whoever believes in him shall not perish but have eternal life"* (John 3:16).

Married couples who make this life-changing discovery that true love is about giving and not getting and put this principle into practice on a regular basis, will soon discover the true secret of sexual intimacy—it is a gift.

Every good, and perfect gift is from above, coming down from the Father of the heavenly lights, who does not change like shifting shadows.

(James 1:17)

Questions to Consider:

1. What are the dangers of withholding sex to get our way in marriage?

2. What would be some useful, biblical guidelines in evaluating whether certain sexual acts are good or bad in God's sight?

3. What part does trust play in allowing the Giving Heart to operate as Christ designed it?

God's Word to Consider:

"Remember this: whoever sows sparingly will also reap sparingly, and whoever sows generously will also reap generously."

(2 Corinthians 9:6)

6

THE ECSTATIC HEART

*Drink water from your own cistern, running water from your own
well. Should your springs overflow in the streets,
your streams of water in the public squares? Let them be yours alone
never to be shared with strangers. May your fountain be blessed, and
may you rejoice in the wife of your youth.
A loving doe, a graceful deer—may her breasts satisfy you always,
may you ever be intoxicated with her love.
Why, my son, be intoxicated with another man's wife?
Why embrace the bosom of a wayward woman?*
—Proverbs 5:15–20

The Ecstatic Heart gives and receives love by reveling in the exquisite pleasure of sharing the sexual act with their life-long spouse.

*If shared pleasures are the best pleasures,
then mutually rejoice in the delights of sex.*

Perhaps the most awkward, yet telling, conversation Bob ever had with his father took place when Homer decided to share his version of "the facts of life." For some reason, Homer chose a car dealership sales lot to have this "father/son" discussion when Bob was in sixth grade. From the very beginning, Bob sensed his mom was behind the whole thing, since his dad was typically quiet and stoic.

A few weeks prior, in front of Bob's older, teenage sisters, his mom had suddenly blurted out, "Has someone told you about sex yet? Do you know how babies are born?"

"Uh, yeah, sure," Bob stammered, not wanting to display his total ignorance. His sisters snickered nonetheless. There must have been just enough hesitation in his voice to convey the truth: Bob was all but clueless when it came to sex.

So as brightly colored balloons tied to the antennas of factory fresh cars danced and bobbed in the wind, Homer proceeded to give Bob the Greatest Generation version of sex.

He began by describing the differences in male and female anatomy in the vaguest of terms. The Dow Jones Awkward Index in the car suddenly spiked. Bob knew his Dad didn't want to be having this conversation. And Bob, for his part, was desperately praying it would mercifully end as quickly as possible. Both knew they were sitting on a conversational dead skunk.

Moving on from Anatomy 101, Bob's father then decided to warn his twelve-year-old son about the dangers of sex. In the Army, Homer calmly explained, he and his fellow recruits were forced to view "training movies" that depicted the various stages of sexually transmitted diseases. Despite what his father might have been trying to say, in Bob's mind, the message was clear: sex would lead to certain death.

Homer further illustrated the point by telling Bob that while overseas, the unit with the largest numbers of newly reported cases of STDs was forced to fly a humiliating purple flag with an eight-ball painted on it. It was a banner of shame intended for all the world to see.

The Point of No Return

With that cheery thought in mind, his father saved the best for last. Without warning, he changed the topic to his own sex life—with Bob's mother. That was it. Bob knew they had reached the point of no return. He seriously considered bolting the car and running blindly out of the lot, hands over his ears, screaming, "No! No! Please, anyone—tell me it's not true!"

But somehow, he managed to stay in the car beside Homer, wondering what bombshell he'd drop next. Then his father said something Bob would never forget, "And men and women both derive much pleasure from doing this."

Suddenly, the fifty-five-gallon drum of awkwardness in the car began to drain away. "Wait a minute," Bob thought as he slowly absorbed the full import of his father's statement. "My parents actually enjoy doing this together." Bob's emotions shifted from fear and dismay to assurance and comfort. "Maybe they really do love each other," he thought. "Maybe they are happier with each other than I ever realized."

Despite Homer's unconventional, inelegant, and convoluted journey to the truth, he had nonetheless arrived where Scripture would have him go. Despite his generation's legendary embarrassment regarding the topic of sex, he had described for his son, in one sentence, the beauty, power, and joy of the Ecstatic Heart.

It was a gift that Bob treasures to this day.

Pleasures that Are Pure

The Ecstatic Heart is an essential and God-given element of a couple's sex life. It enhances their experience in three ways:

1. It causes each person to rejoice in their sexual attraction to their spouse.

2. It gives a sense of intense physical satisfaction as each spouse revels in touching and experiencing their mate's distinct physical features.

3. It offers a continual source of exhilarating pleasure.

Sexual intimacy is intended to produce children and seal the marriage covenant, while also serving as a metaphor for the loving relationship between Christ and the church. God wants a husband and wife to delight in each other as He delights in us. He designed the Ecstatic Heart to provide an ongoing source of intense physical pleasure, free of guilt and shame.

The Ecstatic Heart provides an ongoing source of intense physical pleasure, free of guilt and shame.

As the writer of Song of Songs reminds us with discreet candor, the pleasures of sex are marvelous. Although couched in modest images, Solomon was clearly talking about the physical features of a wife that provide intense sexual excitement to a husband.

> *Your graceful legs are like jewels, the work of an artist's hands. Your navel is a rounded goblet that never lacks blended wine. Your waist is a mound of wheat encircled by lilies. Your breasts are like two fawns, like twin fawns of a gazelle. Your neck is like an ivory tower. ... How beautiful you are and how pleasing, my love, with your delights! Your stature is like that of the palm, and your breasts like clusters of fruit. I said, "I will climb the palm tree; I will take hold of its fruit."*
> (Song of Songs 7:1–8)

The Ecstatic Heart provides for a celebration of physical pleasures too wonderful for words. Yet some couples struggle with the idea that our holy God could also be the Creator of pleasure within the sacred confines of marriage. How could the two possibly go together?

Years ago, a Christian medical physician and his wife, Dr. Ed Wheat and Gaye Wheat, wrote a landmark work on married sexual love entitled, *Intended for Pleasure*.[23] Allow us to quote a portion of their introduction:

> "As a Christian physician, it is my privilege to communicate an important message to unhappy couples with wrong attitudes and

---

23. Ed Wheat, M.D., and Gaye Wheat, *Intended for Pleasure: Sex Technique, and Sex Fulfillment in Christian Marriage*, (Grand Rapids, MI: Revell, 2010).

faulty approaches to sex. The message, in brief, is this: You have God's permission to enjoy sex within your marriage. He invented sex; He thought it up to begin with. You can learn to enjoy it and, husbands, you can develop a thrilling, happy marriage with 'the wife of your youth.' If your marriage has been a civil-war battlefield or a dreary wasteland, instead of a lovers' trysting place, all that can change.

"You see, God has a perfect plan for marriage, which we may choose to step into at any time, and the mistakes of the past can be dealt with and left behind."

Indeed, the Ecstatic Heart finds its fulfillment in the intoxicating experience of joyful physical intimacy with your spouse that God Himself ordained, created, and blessed. The Ecstatic Heart celebrates married physical intimacy as a gift from God.

The Ecstatic Heart celebrates married physical intimacy as a gift from God.

For some tragic reason, many Christians have allowed our sex-saturated and corrupted culture to co-opt the credit for the physical pleasures of sex. It is portrayed as the propriety right of R-rated films, raunchy hip-hop music, and online pornography.

The idea of a righteous and perfectly holy God creating the capacity within men and women to experience the sometimes euphoric physical sensations of the sexual act seems all but sacrilegious if not blasphemous. Sadly, we have allowed a corrupt world to claim the credit for the pure pleasures of sex. The result is a cyber-world with almost four million pages of pornography available for download.

This giving of credit where it's not due has had another tragic result. If this fallen world owns the propriety rights to sexual pleasure, then it can make the rules regarding when and how to experience it. One example is the growing percentage of people, including Christians, who are having premarital sex. The world says there's no reason we can't enjoy sexual pleasure with anyone, whenever we please. If it feels good, just do it. But there is always a price to pay for ignoring God's design and commands. According to the Centers for Disease Control and Prevention, there are dozens of sexually transmitted diseases (STDs) and an estimated twenty million new infections occur in the United States every year.[24]

More and more people are having to confess to their boyfriend or girlfriend that they are bringing an incurable STD such as herpes to their possible future as husband and wife. While it's not an obstacle that can't be overcome, it adds a weight to the couple's marriage God never intended for them to carry.

Those tragic statistics and the immense suffering they represent could be avoided if we would all simply acknowledge that God is the Creator of sex. He and He alone is responsible for all of its ecstatic, intoxicating sensations. In giving mankind these incredibly powerful and exhilarating gifts, He was also very specific about when and with whom they are to be experienced.

Allow us to give our own paraphrase of chapter five of Proverbs, which we quoted at the beginning of this chapter:

> "Satisfy your sexual desires with your spouse, not someone you happen to meet at the gym, a bar, or online. Once you get married, you can continually experience the same ecstasy that you did on your wedding night and you will be blessed with children. Why would you be tempted by anyone other than your spouse? God knows all of your sexual thoughts, desires, and actions, and knows where all bad decisions lead. Any immoral sexual behavior outside of marriage will always be discovered and there will be consequences you cannot control. Your personal integrity and any respect others have for you will disappear. You will be left asking, 'What was I thinking?'"

A shorter version of this portion of Scripture could read, "The pleasures of sex are incredibly enjoyable when experienced with your spouse. And they become incredibly destructive when shared with anyone else."

---

24. https://www.cdc.gov/std/general/default.htm

A Good and Perfect Gift from Heaven

The Ecstatic Heart knows sexual pleasure is a good and perfect gift from the Heavenly Father. He gave it to us simply because He loves to give His children beautiful gifts and see the joy they bring. The Bible tells us, *"Delight yourself in the LORD; and He will give you the desires of your heart"* (Psalm 37:4 NASB).

It should not surprise us when God delights in giving us gifts that delight us. Human parents do the same thing for their children.

One Christmas, our youngest daughter told us that all she wanted was a Barbie House. We knew these houses were expensive and hard to find. But Mackenzie rarely asked for extravagant toys. As a young child, she was content pretending spoons, forks, and knives were her dolls. She would give names to them, create entire families from our silverware drawer, and play with them for hours.

So when Mackenzie asked for a Barbie House, we decided to do our best to make her dream come true. We trudged from one store to another late one cold, rainy, dreary day in December, with no Barbie House to be found anywhere. It was getting late and the sun had gone down hours earlier, but we kept up the search. The fourth or fifth store we went to had just one Barbie House left in stock. We almost hugged and kissed the clerk who emerged from the storage room carrying a box so big, it hid his face.

So why did we do it? Why sacrifice an entire afternoon and early evening to fight aggressive holiday crowds and other shoppers who might want to snatch that Barbie House from us? Why drive through wet, slushy parking lots and get melting white salt on our clothes? Did we believe Mackenzie needed a Barbie House? Were we afraid she'd grow up and fight back tears in a therapist's office some day, recounting her deprived childhood? No. We fought the battles of Walmart, Target, Toy-R-Us, and Value City simply because we loved her (as we do all our six amazing children) and found deep happiness in giving her something that would bring her joy.

Okay, Baby, Where's the Shower?

Cheryl says, "I literally was a baby when I went off to kindergarten. I was four years old and didn't turn five until Thanksgiving.

I loved my teacher, Mrs. Cook, but often wondered if she lived in the kindergarten closet. What did she do when she went in there?

"I grew up in the parsonage, across the street from my school and next door to our church. About every other month, my mom would announce all the church women were gathering at the church for a shower. My dad would stay home with my three sisters and me to make us fudge and popcorn. The fudge never hardened and the popcorn usually burned, but we didn't care.

"Later, I would search the church basement for a bathtub or shower where they had showered. I could not figure out where all those women took their showers when they gathered at the church.

"I want keep my heart and mind childlike, always ready to believe and forgive. I pray I have a soft heart to hear God's voice speaking and see the relationship needs of Bob, our children, and others around me."

The Bible teaches us that God by nature is a giving God. He was never obligated in any way to create this world with all of its majestic forests, azure blue oceans, and towering, snow-covered mountains. Yet He did. As Creator, He could have made food to sustain our bodies without delicious, mouthwatering tastes. He could have made flowers without their aromatic fragrances or stunning colors that would still produce the seeds necessary to reproduce the plants. He could have made dull-looking birds that did not thrill us with their beauty or lilting morning songs. Likewise, He certainly could have created fully functioning human beings with a capacity to procreate without attaching any particular exciting or intoxicating sensations to the process.

But He chose to anyway.

Why? Simply because He loves us. He knew the sacred marital pleasures of arousal, climax, and relaxation would bring added joy and fulfillment to a couple's life together. So we as married couples are free to revel, celebrate, exult, and glory in the exquisite moments associated with sexual intimacy. The power of an orgasm is a gift from above. The exhilaration of joining our bodies is nothing less than a grace bestowed from heaven itself.

And the excitement that comes from viewing our spouse's sexual arousal is a present from a Creator's loving heart.

*God decided sexual pleasure would be
a good and perfect gift.*

From the creation of the world, God decided sexual pleasure would be a good and perfect gift. He withholds no good thing from those who love and honor Him.

The Ecstatic Heart is His gift to us. We are free to give and receive love with the amazing and intense gratification of sexual climax it offers us.

Taking the Name of God in Vain

In return, our Heavenly Father asks us not to misuse His gifts by worshipping the creature rather than the Creator. Instead, we should use the mysteries and joys of sex to glorify God, give thanks, live daily in the truth of His Word, and offer Him eternal praise.

Isn't it sadly ironic that rather than giving Him praise, secular movies, sitcoms, and novels often depict unbelievers doing just the opposite—taking the Name of God in vain during the sexual act? They unrighteously call out His Name even as they indulge in fornication, adultery, or other forms of perversity. As Paul says, this happens because they know God exists, but they neither glorify nor give thanks to Him. Instead, their thinking has become futile and their hearts darkened by rebellion. (See Romans 1:21.)

British playwright Oscar Wilde was widely known for his sexually immoral and indulgent lifestyle. He once boasted, "I can resist anything except temptation!" and "The best way to deal with temptation is to yield to it!"

Yet the English commentator William Barclay quotes Wilde near the end of his life, when he was a broken man and in prison:

"The gods had given me almost everything. But I let myself be lured into long spells of senseless and sensual ease...Tired of being on the heights, I deliberately went to the depths in search for new sensation. What the paradox was to me in the sphere of thought, perversity became to me in the sphere of passion. I grew careless of the lives of others. I took pleasure where it pleased me and passed on. I forgot that every little action of the common day makes or unmakes character and that therefore what one has done in the secret chamber, one has some day to cry aloud from the house-top. I ceased to be lord over myself. I was no longer the captain of my soul and did not know it. I allowed pleasure to dominate me. I ended in horrible disgrace."[25]

Notice Wilde's final chilling words, "I was no longer captain of my soul...I allowed pleasure to dominate me. I ended in horrible disgrace."

Contrast this with the great composer Johann Sebastian Bach, a devout follower of Christ. Even as he penned his glorious music, he would always sign such timeless works with three simple Latin words, "Sola Deo Gloria"—"To the glory of God alone."

The Westminster Confession of Faith says the chief reason men and women were created was "to know God and enjoy Him forever." Yes, sex is intended for pleasure, but a pleasure leading us to know and enjoy God.

The Ecstatic Heart understands that sexual pleasure is a gift from God to be celebrated and embraced by two loving, committed spouses without guilt, shame, or embarrassment. To use it for any other purpose is to mar and distort God's plan for our lives. It's like taking a valuable crystal vase and using it to store lawn fertilizer. The vessel has been degraded not by its nature, but by how it's used.

When we misuse the pleasures of sex,
we are no longer captains of our souls.

25. William Barclay, Letters to the Galatians, and Ephesians, p. 100, http://www.sermonsearch.com/sermon-illustrations/670/paradox-and-perversity

When we misuse the pleasures of sex, we are no longer captains of our souls, but we may not know it until it's too late. And we would end up in horrible disgrace. As the former pastor of Moody Memorial Church, Dr. Edwin Lutzer, puts it, "We cannot manage the consequences of sexual sin. They will always manage us."

The Ecstatic Heart Anticipates a Lifetime of Intoxicating Joy

The Scriptures say, "A loving doe, a graceful deer, may her breasts satisfy you always, may you ever be captivated by her love" (Proverbs 5:19). Two words that stand out for us are "always" and "ever."

God's design for sexual pleasure in marriage does not come with an expiration date like one on a carton of milk. Of course, the day will come when sickness, disease, or death will deprive us of sexual intimacy. Until then, however, we can continually anticipate a future filled with the exquisite moments of sexual pleasure that can transport us momentarily to another place. Or as one husband put it, "She takes me to the moon and back." That is the ecstasy our spouses can bring our entire lives.

The Bible makes an intriguing statement about Moses, the leader called of God at age eighty to lead the Hebrew slaves out of Egypt. He spent the next forty years living in the wilderness, where he received the law of God, set up the tabernacle worship system, and urged the people to trust God and march into the Promised Land. Jewish and Christian scholars alike agree there was no one quite like Moses in all of Israel's history. No one else did so much to shape the character and faith of the Jewish nation and set the stage for the arrival of Jesus Christ as the Messiah.

Moses might be a good example of sexual drive going well beyond age eighty. Earlier in life, Moses had married a Midianite woman named Zipporah. Midian is the land we know today as the western edge of Saudi Arabia. The Bible tells us Zipporah bore at least two sons to Moses. But the Bible makes a remarkable statement that may be referring to his ongoing virility.

The book of Deuteronomy says, "Although Moses was 120 years old when he died, his eye was not dim, nor his vigor abated" (Deuteronomy 34:7

NASB). The King James Version says, *"…his natural force was not abated"* (KJV).

The Hebrew word for "natural force" refers to a branch still green with moisture. Some scholars believe this may be a reference to Moses's virility even at 120 years of age. Moses being sexually active at that age is not impossible. Abraham impregnated his wife, Sarah, when he was 100 years old and, as Hebrews 11:12 puts it, *"as good as dead."* Zechariah and his wife, Elizabeth, were able to conceive John the Baptist though they were both advanced beyond the child-bearing years.

The word "always" used in Proverbs 5:19 encourages us to believe it is not only possible to "always" to be captivated or intoxicated by your sexual relationship with your spouse, but it is a biblical benediction over your marriage that God wishes to fulfill.

Why Is Sex for Some More a Misery than a Mystery?

Let's be honest. That verse from Proverbs may not describe your marriage today. You may have little to rejoice over in your bedroom. You may not have made love for a long time. If sex is intended to be "sheet music," as one author put it, why is it more of a funeral dirge than a symphony of joy? Sexual disappointment and dysfunction may be common in your relationship. If so, you are not alone.

In *Intended for Pleasure*, Dr. Wheat wrote:

> "I think of the woman who has been married twenty-five years and is still not sure what an orgasm is or whether she has ever experienced one…the husband and wife whose egos have been so wounded in the bedroom that they barely speak to each other…the earnest Christian couple who have no serious problems but little joy in their sexual relationship…and many other troubled people whose marriages are filled with misery rather than pleasure."[23]

The Tragic Impact of Past Sexual Abuse

How do couples miss out on the Ecstatic Heart? How does sex become a source of heated conflict and even wrenching anguish?

Near the top of the list of reasons why couples struggle in their sexual relationship is the presence of past sexual abuse in the life of one spouse or the other (and sometimes both). Some statistics suggest that by age eighteen, almost 20 percent of all girls and 5 to 10 percent of boys will have experienced some form of sexual abuse.[26] The support group 1in6.org indicates that more than 16 percent of men have experienced some form of sexual abuse, adding, "This is likely a low estimate, since it doesn't include non-contact experiences and because men are less likely to disclose their experiences due to the stigma, silence, and myths around the issue."[27]

Past sexual abuse can cause spouses to miss out on the joy of the Ecstatic Heart.

Consider the dozens of allegations that have surfaced against Hollywood producers and actors, prominent government officials, television personalities, and others. Many people kept quiet for decades, until the first reports of alleged abuse gave them the courage to speak up. A common theme was abuse of authority.

One woman recalled:

"I was called to meet (the producer) at the Savoy Hotel when I was 17. I assumed it would be in a conference room which was very common. When I arrived, reception told me to go to his room. He opened the door in his bathrobe. I was incredibly naive and young and it did not cross my mind that this older, unattractive man would expect me to have any sexual interest in him. After declining alcohol and announcing that I had school in the morning, I left, uneasy but unscathed. A few years later he asked me if he had tried anything in that first meeting. I realized he could not remember whether he had assaulted me or not."[28]

26. http://victimsofcrime.org/media/reporting-on-child-sexual-abuse/child-sexual-abuse-statistics
27. https://1in6.org
28. http://www.dailymail.co.uk/news/article-4974266/Kate-Beckinsale-Harvey-Weinstein-came-17.html

Sadly, many children and young adults of both sexes do not walk away from such encounters unscathed. When they are violated, they can grow up to view sex as dirty and disgusting, a violation of their personhood. Even if married to caring, kind and considerate Christian spouses, they may at best have trouble enjoying their sexual relationship and, at worst, hate the very idea of it.

We talked to one man who said he divorced his wife because their sex life was nonexistent. His wife had been abused as a girl and wanted nothing to do with sexual intimacy as a married adult. When she would not participate in sexual relations, he divorced her because he believed the situation was hopeless.

There's no question that caring for the heart of a spouse who has been sexually abused requires great patience and understanding. Yet we have seen God bring healing to such people when their spouses are willing to take these steps:

1. Listen patiently and sympathetically to their mate's painful story of past sexual abuse.

2. Identify all of the pain words associated with the abuse.

3. Look into their spouse's eyes and assure them that they care about their pain and only wish they had been there to prevent it.

4. Seek to lessen the pain by living out for them just the opposite of the pain inflicted on them, providing the spouse with dignity instead of devaluation, safety instead of vulnerability, and protection instead of abandonment.

5. Seek out counselors or pastors who can help bring their past pains and wounds to Christ in healing prayer.

Spouses who are struggling with unresolved pain can find it difficult to view sex in a positive light. They know in their heads that their husband or wife is nothing like the person who harmed them in childhood or adolescence, but their hearts are too burdened with fear, anxiety, and emotional pain to trust themselves to anyone.

If your first experience with something God intended to be enjoyable, positive, and fulfilling is instead horrible, degrading, and traumatic, it's going to shape your attitude, emotions, and behavioral reaction for years to come.

This negative imprinting can be true of any painful or frightening childhood experience.

This negative imprinting can be true of any painful or frightening childhood experience, even a non-sexual one.

Cheryl was raised in Detroit across the street from a German Shepherd named Genghis Khan. Every time Cheryl and her sisters walked by, this giant, angry dog snarled, lunged, and threatened to jump the fence holding him back. To this day, Cheryl grabs Bob's hand and stiffens up when she enters a house and spots a dog roaming around.

When Bob was a boy, his rural North Dakota home was hit by a tornado. A few years later, after his family moved to Minneapolis, they spent two terrifying April nights huddled in their home's cement well room while civil defense sirens blared above. More than forty tornadoes struck the city in just two evenings, leaving a wake of horrific destruction and a number of people dead. Today, whenever the summer sky turns eerie colors of green, purple, or dark black, Bob's heart starts beating a little faster.

Early life experiences of neglect, abandonment, or sexual abuse can leave people with feelings worse than these. The wounds can remain well into their adult lives, blocking their ability to enjoy the Ecstatic Heart.

Birdie, Give Me Your Heart

The road to healing for victims of sexual abuse is a difficult one. We want to share the promise of Isaiah, affirmed by Jesus in Luke 4:18, that predicts the future ministry of Jesus in which He will *"bind up the brokenhearted."* There are perhaps few more brokenhearted people than those who experienced sexual abuse as children or teenagers. But listen to the hope God's Word offers to those with hurting hearts:

The Spirit of the Sovereign LORD *is on me, because the* LORD *has anointed me to proclaim good news to the poor. He has sent me to bind up the brokenhearted, to proclaim freedom for the captives and release from darkness for the prisoners, to proclaim the year of the* LORD's *favor and the day of vengeance of our God, to comfort all who mourn, and provide for those who grieve in Zion—to bestow on them a crown of beauty instead of ashes, the oil of joy instead of mourning, and a garment of praise instead of a spirit of despair. They will be called oaks of righteousness, a planting of the* LORD *for the display of his splendor. They will rebuild the ancient ruins and restore the places long devastated; they will renew the ruined cities that have been devastated for generations.*   (Isaiah 61:1–4)

Notice Christ first came to preach good news, the message of the Gospel that we can be forgiven of our sins through the finished work of the Cross. But this passage predicts He would also come to bind up the brokenhearted—that is, heal the pain in our hearts. He came to free those who are captives and prisoners of their past—and that includes sexual abuse. He in turn offers healing and hope, as He bestows beauty, joy and praise on those who have mourned, grieved, and lived in despair for so long.

We have yet to meet a survivor of abuse—including verbal, physical, emotional, and spiritual—who didn't experience a broken heart as a result of their mistreatment. Roberta Parry, in her remarkable spiritual autobiography, *Birdie, Give Me Your Heart*[29], shares the tragic and triumphant chronicle of her life as a child caught up in a foster care system that would place her in seventeen different families before she reached age eighteen.

Incredibly, the worst experience of her life involved a pastor and his wife, who fostered Roberta and several other young girls. He ferociously punished Roberta's slightest infraction, stripping off most of her clothes (sexual abuse) and whipping her unmercifully with his leather belt (physical abuse) while relentless berating her (verbal abuse). The other terrified girls in the room would plead with him to stop (emotional abuse). Following the beating, he would gather all of the girls in the living room and lead them in family devotions and Bible study (spiritual abuse).

---

29. Roberta Parry, *Birdie, Give Me Your Heart* (Mustang, OK: Tate Publishing & Enterprises, LLC, 2008)

Is it any wonder that as an adult, Roberta had difficulty trusting a Heavenly Father? Or why she struggled in her marriage with fear of abandonment and neglect? Or why she couldn't bring herself to leave her own daughter in the care of anyone else? Or why she and her husband struggled in their sexual relationship?

Today, however, Roberta and her husband have a ministry to survivors of abuse. They have discovered that God uses the power of compassion, listening, Scripture, and prayer to mend broken hearts.

They write:

"The Holy Spirit is the leader in the counseling times. When people share with us what has damaged their hearts, we ask for and listen to see if God is showing us something in particular. We put ourselves in their shoes and try to understand how they felt when the damage was happening to them. This is what Jesus did by living here and then going to the Cross. This is why He can be our intercessor and priest before our Father in heaven. The abuse I went through enables me to more easily understand people's pain. We simply take them through the same steps we have gone through ourselves."[30]

Jesus Knows All About Our Pain

It has been our experience that God can heal even the worst wounds of abuse in its many tragic forms because Jesus understands our brokenness. He endured unimaginable verbal, physical, spiritual, and emotional abuse on the cross—perhaps even sexual abuse, since it was common practice for the Romans to crucify their victims naked before the gaping onlookers. It is so vital to our healing that we believe this truth: Jesus understands our pain and suffering. He took it all on Himself on the cross. The prophet Isaiah wrote of the future sufferings of Christ:

Jesus understands our pain and suffering.

---

30. Ibid.

He was despised and forsaken of men. A man of sorrows and acquaint-ed with grief; and like one from whom men hide their face; He was despised, and we did not esteem Him. Surely our griefs He Himself bore, and our sorrows He carried. (Isaiah 53:3–4)

Because Jesus experienced suffering and abuse, the Bible reminds us:

Therefore he is able to save completely those who come to God through him, because he always lives to intercede for them. Such a high priest truly meets our need—one who is holy, blameless, pure, set apart from sinners, exalted above the heavens. (Hebrews 7:25–26)

The night before His suffering and death, He promised us He would send us a Counselor to bring peace to our hearts to replace trouble and fear:

All this I have spoken while still with you. But the Counselor, the Holy Spirit, whom the Father will send in my name, will teach you all things and will remind you of everything I have said to you. Peace I leave with you; my peace I give you. I do not give to you as the world gives. Do not let your hearts be troubled and do not be afraid. (John 14:25–27)

This same Holy Spirit is available today to people who have been abused, devalued, and shattered by others. He will use caring and loving people who listen, show compassion, open up God's powerful Word, and pray expectantly for their broken hearts. He will teach us what we need to know and remind us of what Jesus has said to bring us a peace the world can never offer. Where will He accomplish this wonderful healing? In our hearts—the place God created in each of us to give and receive love.

God Has Made Me Forget All My Trouble

Consider Joseph, a young man found in the book of Genesis who by age seventeen had experienced serious verbal, physical, emotional, and spiritual abuse at the hands of his jealous, unfeeling brothers. They not only mocked the dreams God had given to Joseph, but later threw him into a dry cistern, where he landed with bone-bruising impact. With hearts as hard as iron, they seriously discussed murdering him, but then decided to sell him into slavery.

Those familiar with soul-crushing abuse at the hands of family members can readily identify with Joseph. But God did a remarkable and deep work in Joseph's heart to bring about his healing, evidenced by the names he gave his two sons after he married years later.

> *Joseph named his firstborn Manasseh and said, "It is because God has made me forget all my trouble and all my father's household." The second son he named Ephraim and said, "It is because God has made me fruitful in the land of my suffering."* (Genesis 41:51–52)

Notice Joseph did not say God released him from some of the pain of his past, or free him from most of the torment of his past. Rather, he proclaimed, *"God has made me forget all my trouble."* He also made Joseph "twice fruitful" right in the midst of the land of his suffering. Joseph didn't need to move to another state, assume a new identity, or adopt a new religion to find peace. He found it smack-dab in the middle of Egypt—the place where he had languished in a filthy, dark prison for almost twelve years.

If your marriage and life of sexual intimacy have been hampered or plagued by the impact of past sexual abuse, there is hope. Here is Roberta Parry's closing testimony:

"My heart was able to overcome the world and all that happened to me. I found a dear friend in Jesus. He gave me a new heart and life. I came into a relationship with God who is my Father. I am able to give and receive love. I do still go through trials in life. The difference now is I know where to go when my heart is overwhelmed. I pray that after reading my story, you will be enabled to come to Jesus and give Him your heart. You may come to freedom through a love relationship with Father God. Come, give Him your heart. From this dark world, let Him draw you apart. The Father is speaking so tenderly. Give Him your heart."[31]

Now let's look at another characteristic of the Ecstatic Heart.

---

31. Ibid.

The Ecstatic Heart feels an attraction to the spouse's body as the sole source of sexual satisfaction.

A wise father, perhaps Solomon himself, has good advice for his son, saying, *"Why, my son, be intoxicated with another man's wife? Why embrace the bosom of a wayward woman?"* (Proverbs 5:20). After celebrating all of the marvelous features of a wife's body, he admonishes his son to resist all temptations to turn to any other woman's body for similar satisfaction.

We discuss the importance of sexual fidelity in the next chapter, which examines the Guardian Heart. For now, suffice it to say that virtually anyone can offer you sexual pleasure, but only your spouse can offer it to you with God's blessing.

Anyone can offer you sexual pleasure, but only your spouse can offer it to you with God's blessing.

Attraction Can Bless or Destroy

What a difference attraction to your spouse's body makes as opposed to someone else's. The book of Proverbs says looking at your spouse's body will inspire love, but visually devouring the body of another's spouse will ignite lust. If you delight in the physical features of your mate, it brings you blessing. If you long for another's spouse, you will regret it for the rest of your life. While making love to your spouse can result in a new life, having sex with another is a *"highway to the grave"* (Proverbs 7:27).

Therefore the Ecstatic Heart requires commitment, self-discipline, and the fear of God in order to function as it was created.

The husband and wife must commit themselves to being content with each other's bodies and no one else's. It's a decision to keep the sacred promise you made on your wedding day, "Forsaking all others, I will keep you only unto myself for as long as we both shall live."

Staying Away From the Edge of the Cliff

The Ecstatic Heart operates not only on commitment, but also on self-discipline. While commitment is a choice we make in our hearts, self-discipline is the choice we make in our everyday actions. Micro-cheating—such as looking online to find someone you used to date, or texting a wink to a coworker—is still cheating. The Bible offers this straightforward advice:

> *Above all else, guard your heart, for it is the wellspring of life. Put away perversity from your mouth; keep corrupt talk from your lips. Let your eyes look straight ahead, fix your gaze directly before you. Make level paths for your feet and take only ways that are firm. Do not swerve to the right or the left; keep your foot from evil.* (Proverbs 4:23–27)

Notice all of these commands require a choice on our part, followed by specific actions. We are not to make sexual innuendos or jokes (corrupt talk). We are not to allow our eyes to wander (fix your gaze). We are not to go near foolish places, fill our mind with foolish ideas, or engage in foolish behavior (keep your foot from evil).

The great English preacher, Charles Spurgeon, gave this advice when it comes to avoiding temptation:

> "What settings are you in when you fall? Avoid them. What props do you have that support your sin? Eliminate them. What people are you usually with? Avoid them. There are two equally damning lies Satan wants us to believe: 1) Just once won't hurt; and 2) Now that you have ruined your life, you are beyond God's use and might as well enjoy sinning….Learn to say no."

A Healthy Fear of God Improves Sex Life

Finally, the Ecstatic Heart remains attracted to the spouse's body alone for a lifetime out of the fear of God. Combining the idea of the fear of God and the command to be always intoxicated with your spouse might seem contradictory, but these ideas are cited together in Proverbs:

A loving doe, a graceful deer—may her breasts satisfy you always, may you always be captivated by her love....For a man's ways are in full view of the Lord, and He examines all His paths. The evil deeds of a wicked man ensnare him; the cords of his sin hold him fast. He will die for lack of discipline, led astray by his own great folly. (Proverbs 5:19, 21–23)

Bob once spoke at a church where the previous pastor had fallen into moral failure. The younger, more inexperienced associate pastor there was asked to take on the senior role. Reluctantly, he agreed. After a few months on the job, he confided to Bob, "If I needed the fear of God put in me regarding adultery, I have it now. Sadly, I have had a front row seat to see the sorrow and unending trouble my former senior pastor is going through and frankly, it scares me to death."

Unfortunately, the fear of God is a lost concept in many churches today. Some church leaders think talking about the fear of God and His judgment will lead to empty pews, or they want to avoid messages that make people feel "uncomfortable."

In reality, however, most people want to hear about the fear of God. They want to know about our holy God who loves us, but hates sin, including sexual sin. Accepting the truth and allowing the fear of God to bring us to repentance and a new obedience to God in every area of our lives, including our sexual behavior, can lead to a new sense of freedom and fulfillment.

The seeming paradox that people are drawn to the fear of God and then set free by it was proven in the amazing popularity of an eighteenth century preacher named Jonathan Edwards.

A revival broke out in New England after Edwards preached his famous sermon, "Sinners in the Hands of an Angry God."[32] It was hardly the feel-good talk of the year. Edwards preached to his congregation assembled in Enfield, Connecticut, on July 8, 1741. His basic point was, "There is nothing that keeps wicked men at any one moment out of hell, except the mere pleasure of God." Here are just a few of the "considerations" he discussed in his sermon:

+ God may cast wicked men into hell at any given moment.

---

32. https://en.wikipedia.org/wiki/Sinners_in_the_Hands_of_an_Angry_God

+ The wicked deserve to be cast into hell. Divine justice does not prevent God from destroying the wicked at any moment.

+ Simply because there are not visible means of death before them at any given moment, the wicked should not feel secure.

+ Simply because it is natural to care for oneself or think that others may care for them, men should not think themselves safe from God's wrath.

+ God has never promised to save us from hell, except for those contained in Christ through the covenant of grace.

Historians say this solemn message ignited a spiritual revival that caught fire in the hearts of people from all walks and classes of life. Gripped by the seriousness of their sin and the future terrifying judgment awaiting them, they eagerly opened their hearts to seek Christ as their Savior. The end result was an outburst of joy, blessing, and love that transformed America at the time and for generations to come. Rather than producing irredeemable darkness or hopeless depression, Edwards's message on the fear of God eventually led to countless conversions, healed relationships, restored marriages, and an outpouring of social compassion, including the establishment of new schools, hospitals, and orphanages. This was the First Great Awakening.

Strange as it may sound, the Ecstatic Heart understands and welcomes the truth of Jonathan Edwards's sermon. The fear of God brings the freedom to be attracted only to our spouse and no one else.

Good Fences Make for Good Sex

Think of Niagara Falls, one of the most beautiful and thrilling natural sites in all of North America. When our children were young, we took them to see this marvel of nature one summer. Barricades, fences, and posted signs stop visitors from getting too close to the massive, deafening waterfalls.

Herein is the paradox. The sheer power, thunder, and magnitude of Niagara Falls make them both attractive and dangerous. As we stood less than six feet away from the millions of gallons of water cascading over the precipice, it was frightening to think that just one wrong step could bring certain death. Exhilaration was tempered by terror. Only by remaining safely behind the guard rails could we fully enjoy one of the wonders of the world.

Sex is like Niagara Falls—what makes it so attractive is also what makes it so dangerous.

Sex is much like Niagara Falls. What makes it so attractive is also what makes it so dangerous. Perhaps that's one reason why Niagara Falls was once one of the world's premier honeymoon destinations. Their power seemed like a good metaphor for the power of sexual union.

The holiness of God is also much like Niagara Falls. It's beautiful, powerful, and attractive. It's also terribly dangerous and destructive if it is violated. Stand behind the fences God has established in His righteousness and you can be swept up in one of life's most thrilling moments. Stray outside or beyond the fences and you may be caught in a swift current that will send you plummeting to your destruction.

The Ecstatic Heart will face temptations. Everyone does. Yet the Bible warns us to steer clear:

> *My son, pay attention to wisdom, listen well to my words of insight, that you may maintain discretion, and your lips may preserve knowledge, for the lips of an adulteress drip honey.* (Proverbs 5:1–3)

A Special Sister Shares Her Ecstatic Heart

Cheryl says, "While seminary taught me on one level, my real school for the ministry was growing up with one of my older sisters, Cathryn, who is special needs. She's also my 'Irish twin,' meaning she's only eleven months older than me.

"We liked our teachers, but she loved hers. For her, shaking a maraca was a trip to Mexico and sledding on a cold Saturday afternoon was an adventure on the Swiss Alps. We were glad to go to our church, but Cathy squealed with delight along the way.

"Bob and I have many favorite memories of times spent with Cathy, but one of our favorite times happened one Valentine's Day while she was visiting us. Bob and I went out to get lunch for all of us. When we returned, we got a huge Valentine's Day surprise from Cathy. She swung the front door open and shouted, 'Happy Valentine's Day!'

"She was dressed in red from head to toe. She had on a red headband, red necklace, and red bow. Her shirt, vest, skirt, shoes, and socks were all red. The sweetest thing was that everything was a different shade of red—dark red, pink, ruby, periwinkle, maroon, orange-red, mauve—but Cathy didn't care. It was about love not fashion. She was telling us Happy Valentine's Day with her whole self and wanted us to feel loved.

"Cathy taught me kindness and unconditional love, something that cannot be taught in a book or lecture, but only through the crucible of life by those who live it. I am so blessed to have Cathryn, our gift from heaven, to see more clearly God's heart and ways. She lives out the ecstasy of just being alive each and every day. A hug from my sister is a real hug."

Counterfeits of the Ecstatic Heart

Of course, there are counterfeits to the Ecstatic Heart. The Discontented Heart, for example, is characterized by a perpetual dissatisfaction and displeasure with our spouse and their sexual performance. This inevitably leads to criticism, disrespectful comments, and even contempt.

The Discontented Heart expresses dissatisfaction and displeasure with our spouse and their sexual performance.

Years ago, an acquaintance told us about the conversation that usually took place around his poker table on Tuesday nights. It was open season for men to make fun of their wives. "I'd let you sleep with my wife," one said while dealing the deck, "but she'd really be a disappointment. She's a disaster in bed."

We know another man who returned from his honeymoon only to tell her relatives, "She really has a lot to learn."

It's hard to imagine any spouse making such cruel, insensitive comments, but it's more common than you may think. It's completely at odds with the regular praise spouses with the Ecstatic Heart are to give their mates. Rather than criticizing them, we should follow this advice from Proverbs:

> *Her children rise up and call her blessed, and her husband also, he praises her. "Many women do noble things but you surpass them all." Charm is deceptive, and beauty is fleeting; but a woman who fears the Lord is to be praised. Give her the reward she has earned and let her works bring her praise in the city gate.* (Proverbs 31:28–31)

While we should never discuss our spouse's sexual performance in public, we can allude to the fact we are blessed with a wonderful mate who more than meets our needs. Meanwhile, the Discontented Heart is constantly critiquing and complaining to others about their spouse. The subtext of this criticism is that they may be open to finding someone who's much hotter.

I Can Do Better Than This

Spouses with the Condescending Heart believe they have "married down."

This leads us to another counterfeit heart we call the Condescending Heart. People with this heart believe they are doing their spouse a favor by staying in the marriage. These people believe they "married down" rather than "married up." They point to a number of factors to justify their hubris and arrogance. They may believe they dress better, talk better, and perform better in the bedroom. They see sex not as a loving encounter between two soulmates, but as a contest between two competitors, where only one can earn first place.

Consider the story of John, who had a wife who adored him and three beautiful children. He had married Carrie in part because he had come from a broken home and he was drawn to her intact, two-parent family. Her parents warmly embraced John as their own son and showered him with love and attention.

Over time, however, the unresolved pain from John's turbulent childhood began to catch up with him. His attitude toward Carrie slowly began to change. Where he was once attracted to her emotional steadiness and calm demeanor, he now believed she was boring and predictable. John even began to view Carrie's tender heart as a sign of weakness.

The truth eventually emerged that John had met a woman at work and they were having an affair. Even then, Carrie wanted to work on the marriage and salvage it—at least for the sake of their children. Sadly, John's final critique of Carrie was that he had at last met a woman who made him feel so alive in bed. He chose to walk away from the very home he had once dreamed of having as a little boy and produced yet another divorced home. This is the Condescending Heart—the incredibly prideful attitude that "I can do better than this."

The Foolish Heart has no fear of God.

The final counterfeit to the Ecstatic Heart is the Foolish Heart, which has no fear of God. The Bible says, *"The fool says in his heart there is no God. They are corrupt, and their ways are vile. There is no one who does good"* (Psalm 14:1). The Foolish Heart does not believe he or she will ever be called to account by the Most High.

Answering to God

Hugh Hefner, the founder of *Playboy* magazine, passed away at the age of ninety-one. Part of the supreme tragedy of Hefner's life of debauchery is that he was raised in a religious home. He is quoted as saying:

> "At an early age I began questioning a lot of that foolishness about man's spirit and body being in conflict with God." He went on to say, "Part of the reason I am who I am is that my Puritan roots run deep. My folks are Puritan. My folks are Prohibitionists. There was no drinking in my home. No discussion of sex. And I think I saw the hurtful and hypocritical side of that early on."[33]

Hefner said his parents never told him they loved him or showed him love. He used this hurt as an excuse to objectify women, introduce the destruction of pornography into countless millions of homes, and ridicule the Bible's sexual ethic.

The only antidote to the Foolish Heart is fear of the Lord. *"The fear of God leads to life, then one rests content, untouched by trouble"* (Proverbs 19:23). The sad, certain outcome to rejecting the Ecstatic Heart and recklessly embracing the Foolish Heart is described thus:

> At the end of your life you will groan when your flesh, and body are spent. You will say, "How I hated discipline! How my heart spurned correction! I would not obey my teachers or listen to my instructions. I have come to the brink of utter ruin in the midst of the whole assembly." (Proverbs 5:11–14)

Hugh Hefner will have to answer for the multitudes of men he encouraged to abandon the fear of God and foolishly indulge their sensual desires in the bottomless pit of pornography. How many lives and marriages he helped to destroy, heaven only knows—and indeed, heaven does know. The day is coming when God will judge each of us according to what we have done in this life:

---

33. http://www.dailymail.co.uk/news/article-4928018/The-extraordinary-debauched-life-Hugh-Hefner.html

And I saw the dead, great, and small, standing before the throne, and books were opened. Another book was opened, which is the book of life. The dead were judged according to what they had done as recorded in the books.   (Revelation 20:12)

Go All Out with Your Spouse

Let's look at some ways we can care for the Ecstatic Heart.

If your spouse gives and receives love by expressing the Ecstatic Heart, then you should do all you can to join the celebration of God-given pleasure. As you send the message you are enjoying the intoxicating thrills of sexual intimacy just as much as they are, your spouse will feel loved and affirmed.

However, if you act bored, disinterested, or put-off by sexual intimacy, it will quickly dump cold water on the blazing fires of passion your spouse yearns to experience and eventually put out the spark altogether.

Avoid bringing your latest marital grievances or unresolved conflicts into the bedroom.

Also, avoid bringing your latest marital grievances or unresolved conflicts into the bedroom whenever possible. Certainly there must be reconciliation and harmony for sex to be all it is meant to be. Yet we must be careful not to wound the Ecstatic Heart by acting as if we cannot enjoy sex until every disagreement or dispute has been discussed and resolved.

None But You, Shirley

Another way to care for the Ecstatic Heart is to regularly and openly express your gratitude for the great lover God gave you. Expressing thankfulness openly will keep your heart and mind in the right place. Make a list of all the reasons you are grateful for your husband or wife.

James Dobson, founder of Focus on the Family, wrote this moving tribute to his wife back in 1979 when they had been married for twenty-one years:

"I loved the girl who believed in me before I did…so why do I want to go on living? Because I have you to take the journey with me… to whom will I turn for solace and comfort? To whom can I say I'm hurting and know that I am understood…None but you, Shirley. The only joy of the future will be in experiencing it as we have hand in hand…thank you for making this journey with me. Let's finish it together."[34]

This is the voice not only of a devoted heart, but an Ecstatic Heart as well. A spirit of thanksgiving and gratitude for his wife runs throughout the entire letter. And Dobson read it to his entire staff the day he retired from Focus on the Family. His deep sense of appreciation and thankfulness has turned their marriage into an extraordinary relationship. It will for you as well.

Recall the Joy

Finally, take time to remember the times of exquisite sexual intimacy you've known together. It's a journey down memory lane that may end at a romantic hotel.

Not long ago, Bob had the opportunity to visit the small town where we spent our first year of marriage and finished seminary. One bright Saturday morning, he walked through the neighborhood, which we had not visited in decades. It took a little checking to be certain he was on the right street. Eventually, he found his way to the first home we shared together almost forty years ago.

He stopped and used his iPhone to take a picture of the simple brick ranch house where we spent our first year of married life. When he showed it to Cheryl, it brought back a flood of wonderful and even humorous memories: the kitchen sink that would overflow whenever the neighbors next door did their laundry, the shower stall that was so small there wasn't room to change your mind once you got inside, the heating ducts the landlord had stuffed with insulation that left us shivering to the bone in the dead of winter.

---

34. https://www.oneplace.com/ministries/family-talk/listen/the-dobsons-a-marriage-made-in-heaven-part-1-102357.html

Though we lived in a converted garage for nearly a year none of that seemed to matter. We were newly married and life was good...very good.

As Bob stood in that neighborhood, he gave thanks to God for the beautiful woman he had married and brought into that little house four decades ago. It was the start of an incredible lifetime journey that now includes six children, four in-law children, and six grandchildren. Yet it seems like only yesterday we carried what little furniture we owned into that cramped apartment and set up our first home. Among its many blessings was experiencing the Ecstatic Heart together. All these years later, as the book of Proverbs advises, Bob still rejoices in the wife of his youth.

So can you.

Questions to Consider:

1. Why do you think our Heavenly Father chose to include physical pleasure in the act of sexual intimacy?

2. What are some of the distorted messages that can become attached to sex in the aftermath of abuse? How can the truth of who we are in Christ bring healing?

3. What positive role can the fear of God play in preserving and enhancing the Ecstatic Heart?

God's Word to Consider:

"I have come into my garden; my sister, my bride; I have gathered my myrrh with my spice. I have eaten my honeycomb and my honey; I have drunk my wine and my milk....O daughters of Jerusalem, I charge you – if you find my lover, what will you tell him? Tell him I am faint with love."   (Song of Songs 5:1; 8)

7

THE GUARDIAN HEART

You cry out, "Why doesn't the Lord accept my worship?"
...Because the Lord witnessed the vows you and your wife made when
you were young. But you have been unfaithful to her,
though she remained your faithful partner, the wife of your marriage
vows. Didn't the Lord make you one with your wife?
In body and spirit you are his. And what does he want?
Godly children from your union. So guard your heart;
remain loyal to the wife of your youth.
—Malachi 2:14–15 NLT

The Guardian Heart gives and receives love by keeping vows of faithfulness, protecting oneness, and drawing future generations to God through sexual integrity.

If good fences make for good neighbors,
then great hedges make for great sex.

A Four-Bark Hotel

One of our more memorable overnight hotel stays occurred on the East Coast. We had been invited by a church in Pennsylvania to come for an interview. The church was looking for a new senior pastor and we were considering the possibility of moving from the Midwest.

The chairman of the search committee happened to be an administrator at a Christian college in the area. He arranged for us to stay in one of the college guest rooms during our two days of interviews. The room was tastefully decorated in gray and peach colors, with a comfortable, king-sized bed.

We were sound asleep that first night when the door to our room suddenly burst open. A flashlight was aimed directly at our eyes and then the room's overhead light suddenly came on. Standing in the doorway was a security guard holding the leash of a German Shepherd. (You can imagine Cheryl's reaction if you remember Genghis Khan.) The dog let out a low growl in our direction and displayed rows of sharp white teeth.

We sat up and rubbed our eyes. Was this all just a bad dream, perhaps the result of the overly spicy Chinese food we had for supper? We got a good look at the dog (we later decided to call him Stryker) and realized this was no dream.

"What are you two doing in here?" demanded the campus security guard.

It's hard to put your thoughts together in any coherent fashion when there's a bright, high-powered flashlight blinding you and a dog the size of a horse growling at you—and it's 3:00 a.m.

Then it hit us. Perhaps this early morning drama was part of a secret test set up by the church search committee. Yes, that's right. They were testing us to see how we would perform under the stress of sleep deprivation and an unexpected crisis. Such moments happen in the life of a pastor. Like the Christmas cantata that goes on so long that people slump over in the pews, and fall off into the aisle. Or the guest speaker from another time zone who takes another two hours to finish his message over the grumbling sound effects of everybody's stomachs. Or the parishioner with lethal halitosis who corners you in the hallway to talk endlessly about their recent gall bladder surgery.

Will you stay alert under these dire circumstances and still remember to take an offering? Surely, this was the reason for the room invasion and the canine confrontation. It was a test.

"We are guests of the campus," Bob told the guard while reaching for his glasses on the nightstand. The security guard shined his flashlight back and forth, studying us carefully. Would he believe our story or would he release Stryker to take us out? We suspected he thought he had just apprehended two college co-eds who had snuck into the campus guest house for nefarious reasons.

Stryker strained at his leash. He hadn't had a good bite out of anyone's leg in a while and he was chomping at the bit.

Bob continued to calmly explain that we were there for an interview with a local church. He told the guard the name of the college administrator who had made the arrangements for us to stay on campus. The guard kept his eye on us as he reached for his phone to call headquarters. After a brief murmured exchange, he realized he had made a mistake.

"Um, sorry about that," he said, backing out of the room, pulling Stryker with him. "And I hope you enjoy your stay here. Good night." As he closed the door, Stryker hung his head in disappointment. Another missed opportunity to drag someone to the squad car.

For the record, our interview with the search committee didn't fare much better. Among the strange questions we were asked was, "Do you know what a VCR is?" (This was a few decades ago.) "We'll see you later," Cheryl told one committee member.

"I don't think so," the woman replied with a straight face.

She was right. At least we didn't have to face Stryker again.

The Importance of Posting a Guard

We learned three important lessons from that 3:00 a.m. wake-up call that have stayed with us throughout our marriage:

+ Always make sure your name is on the guest list before you visit a place.

+ Keep doggie treats in your purse or pocket in case you don't make the guest list.

+ Most importantly, if you want to protect something of value, post a guard at the door.

"The condition upon which God hath given liberty to man is eternal vigilance," said Irish orator and politician John Philpot Curran.[35] The same could be said of a married couple's life of sexual intimacy. To protect the integrity of your relationship, you must be forever vigilant. This means stationing a life-long sentry at the door of your sexual relationship.

To protect the integrity of your relationship,
you must be forever vigilant.

The strong word the prophet Micah had for the people of his day can help us understand the vital nature of the Guardian Heart.

It's important to understand the historical context of Micah's riveting messages. The people of Israel were complaining because God was not answering their prayers. It had become painfully apparent God was no longer accepting their Temple sacrifices. To use a term taken from social media, God was "ghosting" them. Despite their many attempts to make contact and get His attention, He did not respond. They were experiencing a spiritual blackout from heaven.

The prophet Malachi was sent to explain why. His message was as simple as it was unsettling:

The Lord is the witness between you and the wife of your youth. You have been unfaithful to her, though she is your partner, the wife of your marriage covenant. (Malachi 2:14)

---

35. https://en.wikipedia.org/wiki/John_Philpot_Curran

The people were recklessly violating the marriage covenant, the most sacred of human bonds. To put it another way, they had broken the Guardian Heart of God. Until they repented of their adulterous ways, they could not expect an answer any time soon. The Lord had them on mute.

The first characteristic of the Guardian Heart is that we forever keep our vows of marital faithfulness.

The covenant we enter on our wedding day is sacred to God, our spouse, family, and friends. In exchange for our pledges of mutual and exclusive faithfulness, our Heavenly Father gives us the marvelous right to engage in sexual intimacy with our new spouse as often as we wish for the rest of our lives.

The door is thrown open wide for a husband and wife to experience passion and ecstasy for a lifetime. Yet God designed this marvelous door to open wide enough to allow just one person to pass through. That person is our spouse with absolutely no exceptions.

Jesus warned, *"But I tell you that anyone who looks at a woman lustfully has already committed adultery with her in his heart"* (Matthew 5:28). Just looking at another person with sexual desire is a violation of our marriage covenant. God's commandment is clear: *"You shall not commit adultery"* (Exodus 20:14). All of our sexual thoughts, words, and activities must be directed only toward our spouse. Allowing anyone else into our hearts constitutes a felony violation of the marriage covenant—a serious problem in the eyes of God.

Love Is the Best Defense...and Offense

So how do we protect the integrity of our marriage vows in a world filled with Internet pornography trolling for the next victim, office orgies on weekends, and a culture that's abandoned all blush at engaging in fornication and adultery?

Joining accountability groups, restricting password access to certain sites online, refusing to download provocative, immoral images, and a host of other external measures can help to guard against moral failure.

There remains, however, an even better sentry to guard the door of our vows of faithfulness. This is the one guardian the Bible says will outlast all others. It will not only protect us from intruders, but will make our lives more meaningful and fulfilling than anything else on earth.

Its name is love.

The apostle Paul makes a bold claim: *"And now these three remain: faith, hope, and love. But the greatest of these is love"* (1 Corinthians 13:13). When time is no more, the universe is rolled up like a scroll, and a new heaven and earth have descended from above, all that will remain of this life is love.

Love is at the core of the Guardian Heart.

Love is at the core of the Guardian Heart. For love will guard our hearts against all the temptations, enticements, and deceptions that sexual sin offers. Praise God there is no temptation on earth that can stand up to the power of love. It can and should protect us even before our wedding day.

Forget black holes, supernovas, and billions of swirling galaxies emitting incomprehensible amounts of energy and light. Forget nuclear chain reactions and weapons of mass destruction. Forget tsunamis, tornadoes, earthquakes, volcanoes, and hurricanes.

Love is more potent, more powerful, and more formidable than all of these. As Paul boldly proclaims, it's the greatest power in the universe.

Why is this so? Because God is love. (See 1 John 4:8.) And God is greater than all of the forces of the universe He created. God's love and love alone can guard the human heart against all of the unrelenting assaults hurled against our marriage by the world, the flesh, and the devil.

Love can rescue your marriage from the statistics that say at least 14 percent of married women and 22 percent of married men will stray from their vows at least once.[36] You don't have to be part of those devastating figures.

---

36. https://www.statisticbrain.com/infidelity-statistics

Just Checking...

Check to see if the iron is off. Check. Check to see if the toaster is unplugged. Check. Check to see if the lamp is switched off. Check. Check to make sure the outside doors are locked. Check. Check to see if the fireplace flue is closed. Check. Check. Check.

Cheryl says, "My mom was a checker. I'm talking she was a triple checker. Her childhood dairy farm home in northern Michigan burned down when she was ten years old. Thankfully, no one was injured, but throughout her life, she was always checking to make sure we were all safe.

"Following closely in my mother's footsteps, I am a triple checker, too.

"The day we moved into our former home, bright red sparks filled a nearby house on the other side of the little preschool park. It looked like a budding fire. At the park, our daughter Megan had met the little girl who lived there, so we raced over to warn them in case someone was in the house with a fire breaking out. In retrospect, I should have called the fire department first.

"Thankfully, but humorously, the huge flashes were coming from their living room pinball machines.

"Do you know how loved it makes your husband or wife feel, just to check up on them? Give them a call when you have a break. Ask them a sincere question with a patient and listening ear. I check with Bob to see how he is really doing, even when I'm busy. I try to ask him just the right questions to get him to open up and express his feelings."

Love Begins with Beautiful Attitudes

So let's get practical. How do we live out this immense power of love in our day-to-day marriage when a child with the stomach flu wakes you up and vomits on your side of the bed, the sump pump quits and you have five inches of standing water in the basement, and your neighbor regularly holds all night beer parties and throws the empties in your yard?

Jesus's Sermon on the Mount and the Beatitudes can become a step-by-step guide to loving God and your spouse in a way that will nurture the Guardian Heart. (See Matthew 5:3–12.)

Use the Beatitudes as a guide to nurture the Guardian Heart.

Each declaration of blessedness builds on the next. Let's take them one by one to see how they can help to make our marriages affair-proof by posting the sentry of love at our bedroom door.

1. Live with an ongoing humility toward your spouse. *"Blessed are the poor in spirit, for theirs is the kingdom of heaven."*

We can become "poor in spirit" when we believe God has given us a spouse far better than we deserve. The more we believe the opposite—the prideful lie that we are in some way superior to our spouse—the more open we become to entertaining small moral compromises. After all, if I deserve so much more, why limit myself to just my spouse? The world deserves me.

Humility produces just the opposite thinking. We realize how unworthy, undeserving, and blessed we are to have this precious person pledge to spend their entire life with us. They also regularly offer their bodies to us in loving, sexual surrender and daily seek our welfare. Such knowledge should produce an attitude of humility and thanksgiving. Such humble love protects us from the dangerous thinking that we have a right to someone else who can offer us better, more exciting sex.

2. Live with genuine remorse over your sins and failures against your spouse. *"Blessed are those who mourn, for they will be comforted."*

We should ask God to let us experience the full emotional impact of remorse for all of our hurtful, damaging words and behavior toward our spouse.

The Bible says godly sorrow leaves no regret. (See 2 Corinthians 7:10.) There are dozens of ways we can wound the heart of our spouse. Harsh words, selfish behavior, and ongoing neglect can leave scars. Yet few wounds are as deep or long-lasting as compromising our marriage vows.

Of course, there is a spectrum of infidelity, ranging from simply looking twice at a coworker with sexual desire to indulging in pornography in the privacy of our home to engaging in a full-blown illicit affair hidden for weeks, months, or years. We were saddened to learn that one of our earlier heroes in the ministry had been involved in an illicit affair for over a decade. Wherever we might fall on this continuum, we need to feel remorse over the pain we have caused our spouse and others. Such godly sorrow fills us with a sympathetic love that can feel their hurt and distress and move us to genuine repentance.

3. Live with patient acceptance through all the undesirable circumstances that may come with your spouse. *"Blessed are the meek, for they will inherit the earth."*

Even when marriage is difficult, we can remain accepting and forbearing rather than turning to another lover for emotional comfort and understanding. (In cases of ongoing infidelity, physical violence, and serious addictions, we strongly recommend that the injured spouse seek the aid of a pastor, counselor, or the appropriate authorities.)

Our spouse may disappoint, misunderstand, or fail us at times. We can expect that. However, countless individuals have found themselves trapped in an affair that started out by simply (innocently?) talking about their unmet needs and disappointments with someone of the opposite sex. Commiserating by the copier machine has led to consummation in a hotel room far too many times.

Meekness is the spiritual antidote to complaining and self-pity over your marriage problems.

Elisabeth Elliot, the famous missionary whose husband was martyred just a few years after they married, once reminded us, "In acceptance, there is peace." When we submit to the truth God is in complete control of our situation, we can accept the difficult times. Hard as they seem at the time, we can find peace in the knowledge they are part of His wise and providential working in our lives. The second verse of the famous Serenity Prayer tells us, "Living one day at a time, enjoying one moment at a time.... Trusting that He will make all things right if I surrender to His will."

This can produce the patient love toward our spouse we sometimes need and prevent us from giving up on our marriage and giving in to sexual sin. We persevere by believing better days are coming and He will one day reward us for remaining true to our vows.

4. Live with an earnest desire to act rightly toward your spouse. *"Blessed are those who hunger and thirst for righteousness, for they will be filled."*

Righteousness in marriage means always asking ourselves, "What's the right thing to do?"—and then doing it.

Hunger and thirst are powerful needs. We cannot live for long without food or water. Jesus said we should hunger and thirst for righteousness in our lives, including in our marriages. We should crave it more than anything else. Thankfully, God is eager to satisfy this hunger in our hearts. He will usually answer our prayer clearly and quickly when we ask Him, "What's the right way to respond to my spouse right now?"

Cliff Barrows, the legendary music director who travelled the world with evangelist Billy Graham, used to say that after a serious disagreement, the nine most important words in a marriage are, "I am sorry. I was wrong. Please forgive me." That's powerful wisdom right there.

God may tell us we need to break off a casual friendship that is developing into something more. He may show us how we have been breaking our spouse's heart with our harsh words or a critical spirit.

This produces a righteous love that seeks to do the right thing regardless of how our spouse responds to us. Righteous love will keep us from straying toward the door of the adulterer should we begin inching toward it due to conflict or disappointment in our marriage.

5. Live with a willingness to forgive and show mercy toward your spouse. *"Blessed are the merciful, for they will be shown mercy."*

Our spouse will hurt our feelings sooner or later. If it happens often enough, we may start to build walls in our hearts and eventually shut them out. We may lose a desire for sexual intimacy with them.

But our Heavenly Father has a wonderful remedy for the toxic chemistry of grudges and lingering bitterness. It's called mercy. Mercy is compassion motivated by love. Rather than keeping a score of offenses, a spouse with mercy chooses to wipe the slate clean over and over again. Rather than seeking paybacks, we choose to give up the right to revenge and retribution. This produces a merciful love that seeks to restore and rebuild after conflict and sin have damaged the marriage. Couples who regularly show mercy toward one another rarely end up in bed with someone else. Mercy slams the door on thoughts of adultery.

Mercy slams the door on thoughts of adultery.

6. Live a life of purity and moral integrity before your spouse. *"Blessed are the pure in heart, for they will see God."*

There is an astonishing amount of emotional, physical, and sexual intimacy reserved for a married couple who have an intense desire for personal purity.

Without it, our view of God is inevitably muddied and obscured. For example, if our eyes are drawn to impure images on the Internet or a billboard, they have trouble focusing on God. Little by little, He becomes more remote and distant to us. When this happens, our hearts are prime targets for Satan's evil arrows of accusation, deception, and temptation to strike our hearts.

When our desire is to live a clean, pure, and upright life toward our spouse, we join God's team in a new way. We soon experience unexpected blessings in every aspect of our lives, including our sexual intimacy. A purity of heart produces a holy love for one another that refuses all sexual compromise. We will be repulsed by the very idea of adultery or moral stains. Jesus will become more real to us than we can imagine.

7. Live with a commitment to make peace with your spouse as soon as it is lost. *"Blessed are the peacemakers, for they will be called children of God."*

Unresolved conflict in marriage opens a dangerous door to temptation while restoring peace bolts it shut.

We must slam the door to moral compromise by facing problems and resolving hurts as quickly as they appear. As one person put it, "We have to open the cage door of the 500-pound gorilla of conflict and let it out." We can't avoid or deny it without risking a more serious problem. We are called to make peace with our spouse just as soon as it is lost.

Peacemaking requires generous portions of honesty, courage, and determination.

Peacemaking requires generous portions of honesty, courage, and determination. It produces a reconciling love that brings you close to one another again, thus protecting you from intruders. Two reconciled spouses won't give sexual temptation a second glance. They are too in love with each other to consider anyone else.

8. Live with a commitment to continue living rightly even when it brings you into conflict with your spouse. *"Blessed are those who are persecuted because of righteousness, for theirs is the kingdom of heaven."*

There are times in marriage, however rare they may be, when doing the right thing actually causes friction and discord.

Your commitment to obeying Christ will require you to say "no" to your spouse—and mean it—if they encourage you to do something immoral or ungodly, particularly in your life of sexual intimacy. Stand your ground. If your spouse insists the two of you watch pornography to supposedly heighten arousal and excitement, absolutely refuse. If they suggest sexual behaviors that you find disgusting and contrary to the model of Christ and the church, have nothing to do with it. If your spouse demands that they be allowed to eat, travel, or spend unaccounted periods of time alone with the opposite sex, at work or elsewhere, you need to draw a red line and say no.

If your spouse encourages you to do something immoral or ungodly, stand your ground and say "no."

Your righteousness may upset them. They may call you extreme or even paranoid. But if their behavior jeopardizes the sanctity of your marriage, it isn't worth the risk. Remaining strong, even under pressure or persecution from our mate, will ultimately bring us God's rewards and protect our marriage.

9. Live with a rejoicing attitude even when you receive hurtful words, mocking behavior, or false assumptions from an unbelieving spouse because of your faith. *"Blessed are you when people insult you, persecute you and falsely say all kinds of evil against you because of me. Rejoice and be glad, because great is your reward in heaven, for in the same way they persecuted the prophets who were before you."*

We are to rejoice even as we experience insults and persecution from our spouse because of our faith in Jesus Christ. (Again, a proper understanding of boundaries in marriage is also required to guard against abuse.)

This can happen when one of you is a believer in Jesus Christ and the other is not. As you attempt to worship Christ as Lord, your spouse may take offense at your faith. They may become jealous of your relationship with God, or accuse you of being judgmental or even fanatical. They may threaten to leave unless they get "old you" back—the person you were before you became a Christian.

Even in such crushing circumstances, where the persecutor is a member of our own household, we are to rejoice and praise God. As Jesus reminded us, others have been persecuted in the past. But our rejoicing love of God will safeguard us against slipping into the tar pits of self-pity, fear, and despair. As we praise God for our hardships and continue to show

Christ-like love toward our spouse, we are shielded from the tempter's plans to push us into revenge mode and find another lover.

Thus, we can see how following the examples set in the Beatitudes helps us to love our spouse in a way that strengthens the Guardian Heart.

What's the Big Deal with Oneness?

The second characteristic of the Guardian Heart is protecting the oneness of our flesh and spirits in marriage.

The prophet in Malachi 2:15 asks, "*Has not the one God made you? You belong to him in body and spirit.*" Other Bible translations render this passage as "*Did He not make them one, with a portion of the Spirit in their union?*" (ESV) and "*Did not he make one? Yet had he the residue of the spirit*" (KJV).

The word that stands out in these various translations is "one." The idea is that God, our flesh, and our spirits in marriage are all wrapped up together. The Guardian Heart protects this divine oneness God has designed into sexual intimacy.

Oneness is a powerful concept, wherever you apply it, even when it comes to food.

Chicago is known for a delicacy named, surprisingly enough, "Chicago Dogs." These are Vienna Beef hot dogs piled high with yellow mustard, a dill pickle spear, sweet relish, sliced tomatoes, sport peppers, chopped onions, and celery salt, all on a poppy seed bun. They all become one with the first bite.

No Splitting the Adam or the Eve

Culinary analogies aside, the Guardian Heart seeks to protect the oneness of a married couple's flesh and spirits. They are not to be split by anyone at any time. Jesus affirmed this everlasting oneness in marriage, "*Therefore what God has joined together let no man separate*" (Matthew 19:6).

A miracle of creation takes place each time a couple marry.

Taking this passage at face value, a miracle of creation takes place each time a couple marry. The service starts with two separate people standing in different parts of the church. The groom is typically in the front of the church while the bride is in the back, waiting to walk down the aisle. However, once they have exchanged their vows and the pastor finally proclaims them wed—"By the authority vested in me, I do announce that they are husband and wife together. In the Name of the Father, Son, and Holy Spirit, Amen"—only one entity walks back down the aisle. A miracle has just occurred before our eyes: *"For this reason a man shall leave his father and his mother, and be joined to his wife; and they shall become one flesh"* (Genesis 2:24 NASB).

Never again will our Heavenly Father look down from heaven and see them as two people going through life. Now in some mysterious way, He sees them as one. Much like the wondrous mystery of the three in one Trinity, they are two in one, never to be divided or split from one another.

Divided We Fall

Many things can divide the God-ordained oneness of a married couple: moral failure in all its various forms; unresolved emotional pain, particularly from past sexual abuse; addictive behaviors; overemphasis on work or career; intrusive family and friends; unhealthy focus on sports or other outside distractions; living out differing faiths and ideologies; and financial problems. That's just to name a few.

The Prepare-Enrich inventory[37] for premarital and married couples lists ten common categories that can negatively impact the oneness of a couple, including communication, conflict resolution, partner style and habits, financial management, leisure activities, sexual relationship, family and friends, roles and responsibilities, and spiritual beliefs.

Is it any wonder that when a test shows a couple arm-wrestling with oneness in most areas of their marriage, their sexual relationship tanks as well?

Let's examine a few of the challenges that threaten to split the Adam and the Eve.

---

37. https://www.prepare-enrich.com

Moral Failure

As we've noted before, few things damage oneness in a marriage more than moral failure. That failure can include premarital sexual involvement, entering into emotional or physical affairs, visiting strip clubs, calling 900 numbers for phone sex, defrauding behavior, sexual harassment, and much more.

Unless moral failure is addressed, confessed, repented of, and resisted in the future, it will do significant and lasting harm to a couple's oneness. Either individually or together, couples should pray to the Lord to cut any negative soul-ties that moral failure has created in their lives.

We are not to yield any territory in our hearts to the devil through our involvement in moral failure. But if we have already done so, we need to take that ground back by confessing, repenting, and resisting all sin going forward. We can then claim the wonderful promise from John:

> If we say that we have no sin, we deceive ourselves, and the truth is not in us. If we confess our sins, he is faithful and just to forgive us our sins, and to cleanse us from all unrighteousness.   (John 1:8–9 KJV)

We heard an effective speaker in marriage ministry confess he had lived in moral failure for almost twenty years of his marriage. Earlier in life, he had experienced a great deal of personal rejection in his family. He had chosen lust and pornography to try to medicate the pain within. He eventually confessed the problem to his wife and the two went to a marriage counselor, who took them through the prayer we just cited. He was wonderfully set free from the guilt, shame, and influence that had resulted from giving the devil "place" in his heart.

The change has been remarkable. Today, his wife frequently introduces her husband as, "The most kind, gentle, and loving husband a woman could ever want."

Resolving the Pain of Past Sexual Abuse

Jim and Diane truly loved one another from the start of their marriage. However, both were raised in dysfunctional homes and had been through a series of hurtful, destructive sexual relationships prior to their coming to Christ. When both became believers, they immediately got involved in small group Bible studies, volunteered at church, and witnessed to their families. They hoped their newfound faith would immediately erase all of the emotional wounds and scars of their past experiences.

However, just a few years into their marriage, they teetered on the brink of divorce. The primary issue was their conflicted sex life. Jim wanted robust, enthusiastic, and frequent sexual intimacy. Diane, on the other hand, drew back. She felt uneasy, pressured, and despaired by Jim's repeated requests. Jim grew more frustrated while Diane became more resentful toward him.

What was causing these two fine Christians who loved Jesus and each other to be so divided in this one area of their marriage?

The answer lie in Diane's past. As a teenager, she had been sexually abused for years. As a result, she associated sex with intimidation, violation, and shame. Even the thought of enjoying sexual intimacy with her husband, kind and caring as he was, caused her to emotionally shut down inside. He in turn felt rejected, humiliated and, above all, angry. "What am I supposed to do?!" he shouted one day. "Find another woman?"

The problems Jim and Diane experienced are sadly common. If your first experience with sex was forced upon you and you couldn't tell anyone—or you tried to and you weren't believed or, worse yet, the person you told blamed you and said it was your fault—you're left with lasting scars on your soul. Simply reciting wedding vows won't fix the problem. There must be a deep healing that only Christ can bring. This healing may take time, so it's important to reach out for help now.

We must point out that past sexual abuse can occur to either men or women. The result, however, will usually be the same. People who experienced sexual abuse in their youth are often angry, confused, or conflicted about sex.

Throughout her marriage, one wife struggled when responding to her husband's request for intimacy. She finally shared her awful secret: she had been molested as a young girl. With tears she said, "Everyone should be able to choose their first time, shouldn't they?" She had been robbed of that choice and it left its deep soul scars.

With the Guardian Heart, spouses can play a vital role in helping their mates heal from the emotional and spiritual wounds of sexual abuse. The wounded person may be carrying so much pain or trauma, they are unable to pray for healing. That requires a loving spouse, trusted friend of the same gender, or a Christian counselor or pastor to pray for them on their behalf.

The Guardian Heart can help spouses heal from the emotional and spiritual wounds of sexual abuse.

In this manner, we come alongside them in their wounds, identify with their pain and, if needed, confess any sin such as bitterness or hatred. There are numerous examples in the Bible of individuals praying on behalf of others using this approach. (See Jeremiah 14:20; Daniel 9:11; Nehemiah 1:7.) Through the help of the Holy Spirit, who is the True Counselor, Christ can minister to a wounded spouse's heart. (See John 14:25–27.)

Depending on the severity of the sexual abuse, it may take weeks, months, or even years for Christ to bring healing, peace, and freedom to a damaged heart. Yet, a caring spouse who brings them to Jesus through prayer can lessen their pain considerably. Furthermore, it will help to create trust in the marriage rather than anger or resentment, perhaps allowing them to eventually experience sexual intimacy as the gift God designed for marriage.

Addiction as the Third Person in a Marriage

Addictive behaviors can also detonate the oneness of a couple. A multitude of obsessions can keep a couple from "clinging" to one another, including alcohol, drugs, sex, overspending, hoarding, video games, excessive cell phone use, and Facebook or other social media.

The problem is, whatever love the addicted spouse may have in their heart goes to their addiction instead. Addicts have a hard time caring about their spouses when they're consumed with getting their next "fix," whatever that may be.

The Dog Under the Table Principle

We were on our honeymoon in Paris. It was a gorgeous moonlit evening as we sat across from each other in an open air bistro not far from the Eifel Tower. A waiter (ah, let's call him Pierre, ma cherie) stood behind the bar, towel over his arm, polishing his glassware.

We looked into each other's eyes across the checkered tablecloth. It was all so perfect: the moon shining over Paris. Two young lovers enjoying evening croissants together. A table literally set for two in the City of Love... Does it get any better?

Bob felt his knee being caressed. His eyes brightened as he looked toward Cheryl and thought, "This is going to be an evening to remember." He squeezed Cheryl's hand as if to say, "Slow down, tiger. The night is still young."

Suddenly, a muzzle appeared from underneath the tablecloth. Bob quickly discovered it was not Cheryl who had been nudging his knee. Attached to the large nose were glowing eyes and a humongous head. We both froze in place. The giant dog emerged full length from under the table. He began to sniff at our plates as if to decide what he would help himself to first—the croissants or the cheese. We looked over at Pierre with pleading eyes, but he just chuckled and kept polishing his wine glasses.

The dog eventually wandered over to another table and we saw our chance to escape the Chateau de Kennel restaurant. We assumed the dog enjoyed a leisurely dessert of crème brulee at our expense and hopefully tipped the waiter. We sure did not. What had seemed all but impossible—to ruin the perfect romantic night in Paris—the Dog Under the Table had achieved.

And so it is with addictions. The dog under the table can be alcohol, prescription opioids, credit card spending out of control, and a host of other compulsive behaviors. If there is a dog under your table, it will eventually impact your life of sexual intimacy. We have known men who became impotent primarily because of alcoholism. We have known women addicted to prescription drugs who are more interested in doctor shopping than making love to their husbands.

If there is an addiction in your spouse's life, there is now a dog under the table in your marriage. Sadly, the overwhelming majority of your spouse's time, interest, and emotional energy are going to their addiction rather than to you.

And if you are suffering from an addiction, restore your Guardian Heart by seeking help from a Gospel-based ministry such as Celebrate Recovery.[38]

...But Names May Never Hurt Me? Not So...

Sometimes, just hearing a certain word like "stupid," "deranged," or "ugly" can hurt because someone used that word to describe you in the past. Of course, we would not use such words to describe our spouse, but we also must be sensitive to the fact that merely hearing them could trigger an emotional response. If so, talking it over with patience, love, and understanding can bring them some comfort and, eventually, peace.

Listen for the gentle prompting of the Holy Spirit. If you're not familiar with the Scriptures, have someone who is a believer and knowledgeable in the Bible pray with you. Together, listen for what God may be saying to you from His living and active Word.

God brings great healing, freedom, and peace when individuals and couples bring their deepest hurt and pain to Jesus in faith. As they listen for His gentle, caring voice, He ministers His Word to their hearts. It is not an audible voice you will hear, but an impression the Holy Spirit will make on your heart. For example, He may bring to mind a Bible verse or story, biblical character, or hymn or praise chorus based on Scripture to bring peace to a hurting heart.

Regardless of how the Holy Spirit may speak to you, it will always be consistent with the Word of God. If what we receive is not explicitly taught in Scripture or consistent with God's character as revealed in the Bible, it should be rejected.

We have seen couples receive much-needed healing and help for compulsive and addictive behaviors when they bring their damaged hearts to Jesus for healing. He ministers His eternal Word to them, creating in them

---

38. http://www.celebraterecovery.com

a peaceful heart free from trouble and fear. (See John 14:25–27.) This in turn strengthens the Guardian Heart.

Broken Chords Will Vibrate Once More

Some time ago, we discovered a little known verse to the much-loved old hymn, "Rescue the Perishing,"[39] which reminds us how God can bring true and lasting healing to our hearts:

> Down in the human heart, crushed by the tempter,
> Feelings lie buried that grace can restore;
> Touched by a loving heart, wakened by kindness,
> Chords that were broken will vibrate once more.
>
> *Refrain:*
>
> Rescue the perishing, care for the dying,
> Jesus is merciful, Jesus will save.

For all the various remedies offered to the addict in our time, we know of none better than those cited in this verse. When Christ does touch the addicts' crushed hearts, those broken chords will again vibrate with love and caring, particularly toward their spouses. The dog under the table will simply go away.

There are certainly a large number of other factors intruding on a couple's life that destroy their sense of spiritual, emotional, and physical oneness. However, it is often not your spouse's personality, habits, or lifestyle that is the primary problem. It's the wall in their heart—and perhaps yours—keeping you from being intimately, lovingly, and powerfully united to one another.

Guard your oneness and watch your sex life reach a whole new level of joy and satisfaction. Couples who experience this deep healing in their hearts often return to our office with big smiles.

"Pastor," they say, "we just enjoyed the best night together we've experienced in years…" At that point, we stop them. Their enthusiasm to share the changes in their sex life that healing in their hearts has brought about often borders perilously on a TMI (too much information) moment.

---

39. http://library.timelesstruths.org/music/Rescue_the_Perishing

Making It Easier for Your Children to Love God

The final vital characteristic of the Guardian Heart is drawing future generations to God as a result of your relational integrity.

Perhaps the most surprising part of Malachi's message to Israel, and to married couples today, is his answer to the question, "Why has God made us one?" (See Malachi 2:14–15.)

We may be tempted to answer, "So we can be happy," or "It keeps us from getting a divorce," or perhaps even, "So we can be a better witness to others around us." There is an element of truth in those answers, but all of them fall short of God's answer. Guarding our marriage is vital because God wants *"godly offspring."*

Guarding the marriage blesses not only the husband and wife, but their children, too. There is a popular attitude in modern society that says we can always find another spouse, so divorce is no big deal. But for our children, divorce is the ultimate big deal. Your marriage may be a trial run for you, but for your kids, it's the one and only chance they get to enjoy the security and blessings of an intact, two-parent family.

Apart from game-changing circumstances beyond your control, such as ongoing infidelity, destructive addictions that a spouse refuses to stop, cruel abuse, or intentional desertion, you need to weigh carefully the impact ending your marriage will have on the most vulnerable, innocent, and trusting people in your life. Reasons such as, "We've grown apart," "We were never right for each other," or "We just can't get along," however true they might be, still fall woefully short of justification for taking a wrecking ball to your children's emotional security, family identity, and sense of belonging.

Children Need Grown-Ups for Parents

Adult behavior is all about recognizing our responsibility to those around us. You may not find fulfillment in your job, but quitting this afternoon is not a wise option, particularly if you don't have another means of paying the mortgage this month. You may find the stress of everyday life overwhelming, but that doesn't justify stopping at a bar on the way home, getting plastered, then getting back on the highway. Your spouse may be more than a little irritating, but that's no excuse for secretly meeting your coworker at a hotel for a little nooky.

The stakes could not be higher. James Dobson, now an elder statesman in the fight to save families, said the most important thing we will ever do on this planet is to raise children who love Christ. Speaking of their eternal destiny, he finished with this somber warning: "Otherwise we will never see them again."[40] This chilling thought should give us all pause. It should also reinforce just how important it is to protect and nourish the Guardian Heart in our marriage.

We met one young woman whose mother brought home an unending series of stepfathers and boyfriends. She told us, "I want nothing to do with God. I don't believe there is one. Religion is for fools and weak people." Had she really rejected the Heavenly Father of the Bible who in love sent His only Son to rescue us from our sins? Or had she rejected an image of God produced by an absentee father who abandoned her at age two and her promiscuous mother who went from man to man?

One hurting husband told us his parents always had their worst fights on Sundays. The verbal firestorm typically started on the way home from church. Noon meals turned into occasions for pans, plates, and silverware being thrown, doors being slammed, and a deadening silence enforced for the rest of the day. As a result, one of this man's brothers got his girlfriend pregnant at age eighteen, one joined a different religion, and a third became a drug addict.

Three of the four Gospels record a serious warning Jesus gave to adults who callously damage the heart of a child:

> *If anyone causes one of these little ones—those who believe in me—to stumble, it would be better for them to have a large millstone hung around their neck and to be drowned in the depths of the sea.*
>
> (Matthew 18:6)

There is an old saying, "The bend of the twig is the twist of the trunk." When our behavior damages a child's heart, it can twist the entire course

---

40. http://www.drjamesdobson.org/blogs/dr-dobson-blog/dr-dobson-blog/2017/11/02/is-your-child%27s-spiritual-welfare-a-priority-

of their life. That's a big deal to God. Jesus goes so far as to say it would be better to us to be intentionally drowned in the ocean than set our children on a path of spiritual ruin and rejection of God. The people we meet in our ministry who cannot or will not pray are typically those whose hearts were broken by self-focused parents who destroyed their security, sense of belonging, and hope for the future.

Some children appear to grow up relatively happy, stable, and unharmed, but emotional and spiritual problems from divorce, abuse, or abandonment often surface later in life. Children of divorced parents are also more likely to see their own marriages end in divorce. *The Effects of Divorce on Children* from the Marriage and Religion Research Institute provides a summary of numerous studies on the subject.[41]

A divorce would impact every person you know and meet, young and old alike.

Suppose you and your spouse don't have children. You may think a divorce would only affect the two of you—but nothing could be further from the truth. It would impact every person you know and meet, young and old alike, from relatives to the children of your friends and coworkers to the child at the grocery store who overhears you saying something nasty about your ex on your cell phone. Your brother who is struggling to hold his own marriage together may decide to throw in the towel because you did. The idea that marriage is not a once-and-done deal would be reinforced for the coworker's preteen daughter who sees you at a company picnic.

Children Are Always Watching and Listening

Little eyes and ears are always watching and listening to how adults treat each other.

Bob once came home with a "Men of Integrity" baseball cap after attending a Promise Keepers event. He wore it proudly till

41. http://marri.us/research/research-papers/the-effects-of-divorce-on-children

one day, we had a disagreement while traveling in our Chevrolet conversion van with our children in the back seats. Bob must have said something short or unkind to their way of thinking because we heard a small six-year-old voice pipe up, "Hey, Dad, what about men of integrity?"

Bob immediately took off his cap. Sensing he was busted, he turned around and said, "Are you saying I said something mean to your mother?"

"Yes," came the chorus of small voices.

"So you think I owe her an apology?"

"Yes," resounded the voices from the back of the van. Bob apologized and put his cap back on.

Yes, we recognize that each person is ultimately responsible for embracing or rejecting Christ. But if we make it difficult for children to experience a loving, tender, and faithful God due to our self-focused, me-first attitude, and scorched-earth fighting with our spouse, then we bear more than a little responsibility for the spiritual decisions they make later in life.

A Revised Version of Malachi's Message

Allow us to offer our paraphrased version of Malachi's message: *Isn't it true God designed you for unity and intimacy in marriage? Your body and your spirits were designed by Him and so they ultimately belong to Him. So why is unity and marriage such a big deal? Because God wants you to make it easier for your kids to come to faith and believe in Him. The more united and loving your marriage, the more they will want that same God in their life.*

While there is a melancholy warning contained in this passage, there is also an enticing promise. If we keep our vows to one another, live in true oneness, and guard our sexual integrity, we will help to ensure that our descendants are drawn to God.

Thankfully, we have seen children of divorce and dysfunctional homes grow up to still love and serve the Lord. We have seen the all-surpassing grace of Christ heal the broken hearts of children who grew up without one parent or the other. We believe there is no hurt God cannot heal.

The Brother Who Appeared in Four Months

Bob's foster brother, Chuck, came to live with Bob's family when he was just seven years old. Bob, feeling alone in family of three sisters, had complained to his parents that he wanted a brother. Four months later, he came home to find a boy his age in his room, playing with his toys.

"Who are you?" Bob asked. "I'm your new brother," Chuck said.

For two years, Chuck's mother came to visit and take him away on weekends, but then, she suddenly vanished. Chuck would not see her again for twenty-five years. Bob's parents offered to let him stay and grow up in their family, so Bob and Chuck grew up as brothers. At times, they confounded their teachers. "How far apart are you two in age?" they would ask.

"We are six months apart," they would reply.

"No, you are not," the teacher would insist.

Although Chuck's mother abandoned him when he was nine, he grew up in a loving, two-parent home, in a family that faithfully attended church on Sundays. Chuck went on to attend a Bible college and later seminary. He has served as a youth pastor for forty years and has reached more than a thousand kids through his innovative outreach youth ministry. Heaven will have its share of men and women who were won to Jesus by Chuck. He is an inspiring example of how a child, by God's grace, can overcome a difficult and painful beginning.

Our Heavenly Father is seeking godly offspring. While it is ultimately the child who must choose what he or she will do with Jesus Christ, we can avoid putting needless barriers and roadblocks in their way by failing to live out the Guardian Heart in our marriages.

Counterfeits of the Guardian Heart

If someone handed you change for a twenty-dollar bill that included three-dollar bills, you would likely call the police to report counterfeit currency. The same concept applies to the impostors posing as facsimiles of the Guardian Heart.

The Careless Heart is reckless in its interaction with members of the opposite sex.

The first is the Careless Heart. It's reckless, often rebellious, in its thought life, words, and interaction with members of the opposite sex. This is the person who ignores the necessary safeguards required to protect a marriage from infidelity or moral compromise.

They fail to put hedgerows or fences around the marriage—mutually agreed upon, steadfast boundaries to protect it. The Careless Heart, if confronted about their irresponsible behavior, will often say there's no reason to worry, they can handle it and, anyway, you are being too legalistic, uptight, or controlling.

Or they display an arrogant attitude that says, "It can't happen to me." They won't acknowledge they are routinely playing with fire. Popular clergy magazines have carried countless stories of pastors who failed to put marital protections in place and lost their ministries to moral failure. "Always stay behind the desk" is one caution pastors need to heed.

This is why personal accountability is so vital. We know several pastors who wisely hire administrative assistants of the same sex to travel with them. Their churches pay for the assistants' expenses when the pastors must journey to other cities to share their ministries. When someone travels with you, you're far less likely to make a foolish choice in what you watch, where you go, or who you talk to alone.

The Modesto Manifesto

The beloved late evangelist Billy Graham was consistently listed as one of the Most Admired Men in America during much of his remarkable fifty-year career. As a thirty-one-year-old husband and father, when his public fame was skyrocketing, he and his associates became worried they would commit a financial misstep or moral mistake that would ruin their reputations and thus end their ministry.

They gathered in a motel room in Modesto, California, and drew up what would later be known as the Modesto Manifesto. *Christian History* magazine gives us some of the details of their self-imposed decision to build hedges around their marriages, finances, and public ministry:

> "Nothing loomed larger than sex. The most famous provision of the manifesto called for each man on the Graham team never to be alone with a woman other than his wife. Graham, from that day forward, pledged not to eat, travel, or meet with a woman other than Ruth unless other people were present. This pledge guaranteed Graham's sexual probity and enabled him to dodge accusations that have waylaid evangelists before and since."[42]

Graham would later reveal in his best-selling autobiography, *Just as I Am*, why he and his team took such bold steps to safeguard their lives from scandal:

> "We all knew of evangelists who had fallen into immorality while separated from their families by travel. We pledged among ourselves to avoid any situation that would have even the appearance of compromise or suspicion. From that day on, I did not travel, meet or eat alone with a woman other than my wife. We determined that the Apostle Paul's mandate to the young pastor Timothy would be ours as well: 'Flee...youthful lusts' (2 Timothy 1:22, KJV)."[43]

Graham's attitude was just the opposite of the Careless Heart.

Build hedges to safeguard your marriage.

---

42. https://christianhistoryinstitute.org/magazine/article/the-modesto-manifesto/
43. Billy Graham, *Just As I Am: The Autobiography of Billy Graham* (New York: HarperCollins Publishers, 1997)

There are other safeguards we can take to protect the Guardian Heart. Some ideas are ours; some are borrowed from the excellent book, *Hedges: Loving Your Marriage Enough to Protect It.*[44] Those safeguards should include:

+ Not sharing intimate details of our life or marriage in conversation with members of the opposite sex

+ Turning off or closing out of all online media the moment it becomes sexually suggestive or explicit

+ Copying our spouse on all emails or text messages sent to members of the opposite sex who are not our relatives

+ Giving our spouse full access to all of our online technology, history, passwords, and phone numbers

+ Not engaging in online social media relationships with members of the opposite sex apart from involving our spouse

+ Using great caution when displaying physical touch with members of the opposite sex, such as a hug, a kiss on the check, or a touch on the arm, and doing so only in the presence of our spouse or others

+ Keeping our spouse close by at parties, social events, class reunions, and other events or outings

+ Listening to our spouse's warning and taking appropriate action when they detect someone of the opposite sex showing unusual or special interest in us

Open to a Better Deal

Another counterfeit to the Guardian Heart is the Open to a Better Deal Heart.

The Open to a Better Deal Heart is
on the look-out for other options.

---

44. Jerry B. Jenkins, *Hedges: Loving Your Marriage Enough to Protect It* (Wheaton, IL: Crossway Books, 2005)

Those with this heart keep their promises of sexual fidelity as long as it serves their purposes. Once they find someone more emotionally or physically attractive, they are willing to explore that option. Rather than falling into moral sin through a careless lack of hedges, these individuals are actually on the look-out for someone else to fulfill their sexual fantasies and desires. If a better deal comes along, they may decide to take it.

Some suggest that up to 20 percent of all men enrolled on prominent Internet match-making websites are married men posing as singles. Some dating websites such as AshleyMadison.com skip the pretense of singleness altogether and openly present a forum for people wanting to commit adultery. This is the Open to a Better Deal Heart on steroids.

Recognizing the Great Deception

Despite the dishonesty, betrayal, and lasting damage that such a promiscuous heart does to innocent spouses, it's all based on the great deception. It's the belief that somehow, illicit sexual intimacy will at last fulfill a person's deep need for love, and acceptance.

As psychologists Dr. Henry Cloud and Dr. John Townsend point out:

"Each of us has different desires and wants, dreams and wishes, goals and plans, hungers and thirsts. We all want to satisfy 'me.' But why are there so few satisfied 'me's' around? Part of the problem lies in the lack of structured boundaries within our personality. We can't define who the real 'me' is and what we truly desire. Many desires masquerade as the real thing. They are lusts that come out of now owning our real desires. For example, many sex addicts are looking for sexual experiences, but what they really desire is love and affection."[45]

What the Open to a Better Deal Heart often learns too late is that he or she was really looking for genuine love rather than just another sexual zing. It's like a person at the state fair who buys cotton candy for lunch instead of a grilled chicken sandwich. An hour later, his gut tells him he traded real nutrition for a sugar crash and emptiness.

---

45. Henry Cloud, and John Townsend, *Boundaries* (Grand Rapids, MI: Zondervan, 1992)

The writer of Proverbs warns us:

For the lips of the adulterous woman drip honey, and her speech is smoother than oil; but in the end she is bitter as gall, sharp as a double-edged sword. Her feet go down to death; her steps lead straight to the grave. (Proverbs 5:3–5)

We Are Made for Real Love

The real key to breaking free from the Open to a Better Deal Heart is to open your heart to real love—the love God and your spouse have for you. You need to let their love flow in and flow out. This is what we were made for when we were made in the image of God—to give and receive love from our hearts.

Cloud and Townsend write that we are indeed made for genuine love, not the counterfeit varieties:

"Our ability to give and respond to love is our greatest gift. The heart that God has fashioned in His image is the center of our being. Its abilities to open up to love and to allow love to flow outward are crucial to life. Many people have difficulty giving and receiving love because of hurt and fear. Having closed their heart to others they feel both empty and meaningless. The Bible is clear about both functions of the heart: the receiving of grace and love inward and the flow outward."[46]

The truth is, the better deal never actually comes along because the Open to a Better Deal Heart is based on selfishness and dishonesty rather than self-giving love and integrity. A seasoned pastor told Bob, "My father once told me any woman willing to have sex with you outside of marriage wasn't worthy of you. I listened to my father and have never regretted it."

Talking to Others, Planting Hedges and Showing PDA

We'd like to offer a few other suggestions on caring for the Guardian Heart.

---

46. Ibid.

First, continually express to your spouse that you have an unwavering, lifelong, ironclad commitment to your marriage vows. This is most effective when done in the presence of others, particularly parents, friends, or coworkers. To make your marriage especially affair-proof, always say positive things about your spouse in front of coworkers. The message you send will be unmistakably clear: you love your spouse, are delighted with your marriage and have zero interest in anyone else. It's funny how temptation will seem to skip over you when you are vocally and unmistakably clear that you are married for life.

Second, not only plant hedges around your relationship, but keep them trimmed. Take the time to discuss with your spouse how well your current fences are working. Are there gaps in the bushes that could lead to trouble some day? Are additional trees needed due to changing circumstances? Review the last year and celebrate together how your hedges have worked to safeguard your marriage. Each victory we achieve sets the stage for the next one.

Third, remember that sexual integrity and purity in marriage are best safeguarded by an attitude of humility that says, "It could happen to me," rather than, "I'm way beyond that." Pride does go before a fall and a haughty spirit before a downfall, Proverbs 16:18 warns. A healthy fear of sin and a profound distrust of your sinful human nature can together go a long way to keep your marriage vows intact.

Finally, let your children regularly see your tender love and affection for one another.

Children have a love/hate attitude when it comes to witnessing their parents' public displays of affection (PDAs). On the one hand, they are mortified by the idea their parents may actually have sex. Sure, kids may know how babies are made, but they often think sex is an occasional yucky thing parents do just so they can have kids. As radio talk show host Dave Ramsey says, "Our parents never talked about money or sex with us. We didn't think they had either. It turns out they had both."

On the other hand, children are secretly thrilled when they see mom and dad hug, kiss, and act like they're in love. It envelops their hearts with a blanket of security. As long as they live, they need reassurance that the union that brought them into existence is still strong and unbreakable.

Lessons from Katie the Lion-Hearted

For many years, we were blessed with a smaller than usual but sweeter than most Labrador Retriever named Katie. Although half the size of a normal yellow Lab, what she lacked in stature, she made up for in spunk and spirit.

Katie always surprised us with her antics. When family members phoned, she listened to our conversation with sincere interest. If you talked about another dog in front of her, she whined. It seemed she was truly jealous.

One day, Katie ran into living room and jumped on to the couch—and her paw landed on the remote control, which turned on the wide-screen TV. Instantly, she sat down to watch. We were surprised, but she apparently was channel surfing for Animal Planet.

As for being an expert watchdog, that's a different story. Legendary for her barking, she barked at us, her own family, every time we came in the front door from outside. It didn't matter who pulled into the driveway. As soon as she heard the crunch of tires, she sprang into action. She started barking as if the house was on fire and her tail was already smoking. She'd run to the front door or jump on to the bay windowsill and bark unceasingly until we entered the room and told her to stop.

What she lacked in discretion regarding friend or foe she more than made up for in guarding our family with all her might. Although a back injury ended her sweet and loyal life prematurely, we all learned a valuable lesson from Katie the Lion-Hearted: if you have the Guardian Heart, you will challenge and chase away any and every would-be intruder who would threaten your home—or marriage.

So may it be with you.

Questions to Consider:

1. If our love is strong and our marriage commitment sincere, do we still need to post a guard at the door of our bedroom?

2. How does living a life of love modeled after the Beatitudes protect a couple from violating their marriage vows?

3. What impact does genuine oneness in marriage have on our children's ability to believe there is a loving and caring God in heaven?

God's Word to Consider:

"Now then, my sons, listen to me; do not turn aside from what I say. Keep to a path far from her, do not go near the door of her house, lest you give your best strength to others and your years to one who is cruel, lest strangers feast on your wealth and your toil enrich another man's house. At the end of your life you will groan, when your flesh and body are spent." (Proverbs 5:7–11)

8

THE HEART OF THE SIX HEARTS

For God so loved the world that he gave his one and only Son,
that whoever believes in him shall not perish but have eternal life.
—John 3:16

After reading this book you may be thinking, "Okay, I can identify with one or more of the Six Hearts of Intimacy. I can even see how these Six Hearts are key to a great sex life in our marriage. But how in the world can I find the strength and willingness and love to live these out in my marriage?"

The answer can be found in the Gospel of Jesus Christ.

Who's Driving Your Car?

Cheryl remembers, "I trusted in Christ alone for my salvation when I was six years old. Later in high school and college, I pushed Him into the back seat and took over the steering wheel of my life. When I was going back to college after Christmas break senior year, from Flint, my friends and I had to drive four hours south to Indiana.

"I had known these girls since childhood in eastern Michigan and we were now suite-mates. Unfortunately, we were in the middle of a huge blizzard. As we tried to drive along, I was verbalizing my fear of crashing and dying. A friend who was a year younger, but much wiser, challenged me, saying although she didn't like the bad weather conditions either, she had peace because she knew God had everything under control and she was in His hands. Paula's words pierced me because I had 'the wheel' to my life, not God.

"While the truth from a friend stings at first, it was the truth. We couldn't even see out of the car because of the swirling snow squall, so I closed my eyes, trusted Christ, and gave the idols in my life back over to Him. I have known hundreds who were desperately sorry at the end of their life that they did not follow Christ all their days, but I have never known anyone who followed Christ sorry that they did. Christ will save you even at the last minute, but don't count on having that last minute.

"Do you want to know peace in Christ? Pray the prayer at the end of this chapter. If you are headed the wrong way, God can turn your car in the opposite direction. *'Indeed, I count everything as loss because of the surpassing worth of knowing Christ Jesus my Lord'* (Philippians 3:8)."

The Gospel gives us the power, ability, and desire to shift our focus from ourselves to another person and their needs. *"Do nothing out of selfish ambition or vain conceit,"* writes the apostle Paul. *"Your attitude should be the same as that of Christ Jesus"* (Philippians 2:3, 5).

Trust Jesus to Strengthen the Romantic Heart

Allow us to illustrate. Let's start with the Romantic Heart. When we are tired, worn-out, or even upset by life or our spouse, romance might be the last thing on our mind. Why should I take time to lovingly gaze into their eyes, whisper into their ear, or plan for some quality time alone together when the baby just kept us up all night? Or I have to get a second job to pay some unexpected bills? Or my spouse forgot our anniversary?

The Gospel teaches us Jesus came not to be served, but to serve. He used His divine power only to benefit others, never Himself. Even in His final hours on the cross, He used His remaining strength to care for others. (See John 19:26–27.)

That same unselfish and caring Jesus can give you the strength and desire to romance your spouse even when you don't feel like it. Such romance can reignite sexual intimacy and joy in your marriage. Try this prayer:

> "Lord Jesus, fill me with a desire to offer my spouse romantic love. Let me desire again to bond with my eyes, use words to stir their imagination, and make time for us to be alone together. Do all this in and through me as you turn my weakness into strength and my empty heart into one overflowing with new love. Amen."

God's Presence Renews the Worshipping Heart

Or consider the Worshipping Heart. How can we exalt God's presence in our sexual relationship, demonstrate sacrificial love, and show extraordinary honor when we don't even like each other at the moment? Again, we look to Jesus for answers. Jesus lived every moment of every day with an awareness of God's Presence in His life. He said:

> Don't you believe that I am in the Father, and that the Father is in me? The words I say to you I do not speak on my own authority. Rather, it is the Father, living in me, who is doing his work.   (John 14:10)

The realization that God the Father was present with Him gave Jesus the ability to sacrificially love the unlovable and show extraordinary honor to those who knew nothing but dishonor. When we are feeling discontented, discouraged, and depressed in marriage, we can find new strength to live out the Worshipping Heart by believing the promise of Christ: "*Never will I leave you, never will I forsake you*" (Hebrews 13:5).

We can stop our downward spiral when we lift up God's presence with praise and thanksgiving. For the Bible tells us, "*God inhabits the praise of His people*" (Psalm 22:3). Listen to some inspiring praise music on your iPhone. Sit outside, close your eyes, and let the Presence of Christ wash over your soul. Read the Bible and let God connect with your heart in a fresh way. Soon, your Worshipping Heart will be beating strong. That fresh sense of God's presence can reignite our desire to show love and honor to our spouse. One result will be a renewed sexual attraction and desire for intimacy.

Jesus Is a Model for the Companion Heart

Or what of the Companion Heart? How do we develop and maintain deep soul ties, emotional camaraderie, and undying loyalty to one another through all the changing seasons of life? It can be easy when you're young and energetic, but what happens when the years go by and your teenagers start to rebel, your finances crash, or you develop health problems that become a constant source of concern?

Be My Friend and I'll Give You a Soda

Cheryl recalls, "The first day of middle school, you couldn't see a blade of grass on our lawn because of all the kids who showed up to walk with RJ. His friendship was a form of protection and credentials for a cool reputation. Kids wanted a companion they could count on.

"RJ made and kept friends easily, though at times, he made some dubious promises. For example, he was elected to student council in fifth grade with a campaign promise to bring soda machines onto campus. RJ kept his campaign promise by smuggling twelve-packs from home into his locker to sell at a huge profit."

When life's problems and pressures hit you like a piano dropped from ten stories above, how do you and your spouse stay best friends? How do you cope and keep the Companion Heart alive when the temptation becomes strong to blame one another for life's cruel heartaches and crushing sorrows?

Again, we can turn to the Gospel for assistance. As the song from a different generation reminds us, "What a friend we have in Jesus, all our sins and griefs to bear..." Notice the writer divides our problems into two categories: sin and pain. The same two categories, we believe, damage every heart.

Jesus said:

I no longer call you servants, because a servant does not know his master's business. Instead, I have called you friends, for everything that I learned from my Father I have made known to you.   (John 15:15)

Knowing Jesus is our constant friend and companion, we can find the motivation to be the same to our spouse. As the Companion Heart finds new life and breath in your marriage, it will draw you back together, rekindling your sexual relationship.

God's Love Fuels the Giving Heart

What about when you're tired of giving, or as one pop song puts it, you feel like your spouse is "all taking and no giving"? How can you think about unselfishly responding to their needs and lovingly surrendering your body with the Giving Heart when it seems like your marriage has become a one-way street? When it seems like you spend your whole day thinking about what they want next, what their needs are, and how to make them happy? You end up exhausted, frustrated, and angry.

It could be things are out of balance and your relationship problems need to be addressed. Yet the answer is not to become a taker yourself and demand that your spouse do all the giving for a change. Rather, you both need to rediscover the power of the Gospel and create in both of you the Giving Heart.

No one ever lived a more unselfish life than Jesus Christ. He sets a beautiful example for us to follow. *"It is more blessed to give than receive"* (Acts 20:35) takes on new power and meaning.

Count the number of times Jesus uses the word "give," "gave," or "gift" in the Gospels and you quickly begin to see that the Giving Heart is the heart of our Savior. Jesus told the woman at the well in John 4:10, *"If you knew the **gift** of God and who it is that asks you for a drink you would have asked Him and He would have **given** you living water."* Again, some of the gospel hymns have remarkably good theology and practical advice for living the Christian life.

Consider this powerful reminder of the limitless well of God's giving grace from songwriter Annie J. Flint:

"When we have exhausted our store of endurance, when our strength has failed (and) the day is half done, when we reach the end of our hoarded resources Our Father's full giving is only begun....His love has no limits, His grace has no measure, His power no boundary known unto men; For out of His infinite riches in Jesus, He giveth, and giveth, and giveth again."[47]

When we are wrung out and don't feel like giving anything, particularly when our spouse suggests we have sex, it's at that very moment we can look to the Gospel and out of His infinite riches, God can give us the grace to give once again. Remember, the love of the indwelling Christ has no limits, His grace has no measure, and His power has no boundaries. When we ask Jesus to give us His Giving Heart, it can light a new flame of passion between us. We suddenly find the grace to offer to our spouse what they truly need from us, including sexual intimacy and fulfillment.

Freed From the Past, We Can Embrace the Ecstatic Heart

How can we revel in the passion and pleasures of the Ecstatic Heart when we are burdened by past guilt, shame, and lack of desire? Perhaps our sexual sins of the past keep reminding us of our failures. Or the voice of the enemy taunts us with the idea that we are permanently damaged goods. Again, we look to the Gospel and the finished work on the cross for the answer. Isaiah tells us how Jesus offers to exchange our long list of sins and receive in return His blank sheet of a spotless life:

Surely he took up our pain and bore our suffering, yet we considered him punished by God, stricken by him, and afflicted. But he was pierced for our transgressions, he was crushed for our iniquities; the punishment that brought us peace was on him, and by his wounds we are healed. We all, like sheep, have gone astray, each of us has turned to our own way; and the LORD has laid on him the iniquity of us all.

(Isaiah 53:4–6)

---

47. http://library.timelesstruths.org/music/He_Giveth_More_Grace

When we know we are free from all the condemning sins of the past and declared not guilty by Christ, we can freely and joyfully enter into the full passion and pleasures of married sexual intimacy. Then the intoxicating love of our spouse can fan the Ecstatic Heart into a full blaze once again.

The Trinity Bears the Gift of the Guardian Heart

Finally, how do we live out the Guardian Heart when we are caught up in an evil-for-evil marital relationship, involved in ungodly behaviors, or face unacknowledged addictions that threaten to divide our oneness as a couple? What happens when these divisions threaten to embitter our children toward God? Where do we go when we no longer feel like keeping the vows we made years ago?

Again, we turn to the message of the Gospel. The Bible promises that the Heavenly Father can make us one, even as the Father, Son, and Holy Spirit are one.

On the last night of His life, Jesus prayed to His Father:

I pray also for those who will believe in me through their [the disciples'] message, that all of them may be one, Father, just as you are in me and I am in you. May they also be in us so that the world may believe that you have sent me.   (John 17:20–21)

A Family United for All Eternity

We think the gates of heaven must be even more beautiful than France's Eiffel Tower, constructed as the entrance to the 1889 World's Fair.

Gates always played an important role when Bob's extended family went anywhere. When meeting at Disneyland, Chicago's Shedd Aquarium, or an amusement park, Bob's mother would always say, "Meet Dad and me just inside the gate." And sure enough, there she would be, smiling broadly, arms wide open, waving at her kids and grandkids. Several relatives talked about these occasions at her funeral. "We'll meet you, Grandma, just inside the gates of heaven," they promised her.

When we trust in Christ, He pays the penalty for all of our sins. May the Eiffel Tower remind you that you will be reunited with your dear family someday, as they wait for you just inside heaven's gates.

The unity, love, and respect that exists in the Trinity is something God wishes to share with everyone who will believe the message of the Gospel. Division is of the devil; unity is of God. This simple truth can transform a couple's marriage and rebuild the hedges of the Guardian Heart. As we return to an exclusive, life-long commitment to sexual integrity, the pay-offs in renewed trust and sexual fulfillment will begin almost immediately. Perhaps best of all, we will have bound up our children's hearts and clear the way for them to place their faith in a loving God who brings unity to our hearts and homes.

If you have failed your children through your anger, arguments, and division as a couple, it's not too late. Go back to them one by one and confess:

"I have been wrong in how I have treated your (mother or father). I have failed to show them the love of Christ. Instead, I have acted selfishly and unlovingly toward them. I know our fighting and arguments have damaged your heart. I am deeply sorry for my actions. I wish to make things right with God, your (mother/father), and with you. Will you allow me to regain your trust? Will you forgive me?"

We cannot say for certain how your child will respond. But you will have opened the door to restoration and healing. Who knows where it will lead? If you are sincere in your apology and let the Gospel of Jesus Christ create a new Companion Heart in you, don't be surprised if your children one day return to Him or claim Him as their own Savior.

Still the One

Bob says, "It's been four decades since I first spotted Cheryl in the hallways of school and later stood on a cafeteria table pretending to be Billy Graham to get her attention. She is still the lovely, talented, and incredibly outgoing person who attracted me in the first place. She has faithfully supported me in my desire to see hearts healed and marriages restored, particularly in under-served communities. She has sacrificed much, worked endless hours, and lived by faith while continuing to believe God called us to this work. Better still, she has lived out each of the Six Hearts of Intimacy in our marriage for all the years God has allowed us to walk life's journey together. May I say to Cheryl, 'I owe you so much, I thank you, and I love you.'"

God Can Make You a Perfect Match

A few years ago, a popular Southern Gospel music couple, Pastor Norman Hutchins and his wife, Karen, discovered he was suffering from acute kidney failure.[48] If he did not find an exact donor match soon, his prospects for living much longer were grim indeed.

To everyone's amazement, his wife was the ideal match for a kidney transplant. The chances that she would be the perfect donor were one in 2.5 million. Yet she was—and without hesitation, she freely offered one of her kidneys to save her husband's life.

The power of the Gospel can make your hearts a perfect match for one another. Your life, your marriage, and even your experience of physical intimacy as spouses will be forever changed. The Gospel will give you the power, ability, and desire to love each other as Christ loves us.

A Prayer for a New Life

Have you received the gift of eternal life that Jesus Christ offers? If not, why not pray this simple prayer and begin an entirely new adventure in your life and marriage?

Dear Jesus, I recognize that I have sinned and fallen short of the glory of God. I understand there is nothing I can do to earn or deserve Your salvation. I choose to repent of my unbelief and sin. I place my faith in the finished work of the cross where You, Jesus, shed Your blood as payment for my sins. I receive Your free gift of eternal life and acknowledge You as my Savior and Lord. Thank

48. http://pathmegazine.com/news/gospel/norman-hutchins-wife-gives-gospel-legend-kidney-pastor-hutchins-later-flatlines-on-hospital-bed/

You that as many as believe on Your name, You give the right to become children of God. I believe in that Name and ask You to fill me with Your Holy Spirit. Empower my life to love, obey, and trust You for the rest of my days. Thank You for the gift of eternal life that is now mine. In Jesus's Precious Name, Amen.

May Christ give you the ability to give and receive love through the Six Hearts of Intimacy.

He designed each one with you in mind.

Love is patient, love is kind. It does not envy, it does not boast, it is not proud. It does not dishonor others, it is not self-seeking, it is not easily angered, it keeps no record of wrongs. Love does not delight in evil but rejoices with the truth. It always protects, always trusts, always hopes, always perseveres. Love never fails. (1 Corinthians 13:4–8)

Questions to Consider:

1. Why is the Gospel of Jesus Christ the most important element in living out the Six Hearts of Intimacy in our marriage?

2. What are some common substitutes that people use to try to make their life of sexual intimacy work?

3. How can the truth that *"God so loved the world that He gave His One and Only Son..."* serve as a model for us in loving our spouse?

God's Word to Consider:

> *"My command is this: Love each other as I have loved you. Greater love has no one than this, that he lay down his life for his friends."*
>
> (John 15:12–13)

Appendix

SELF-TEST FOR
THE SIX HEARTS OF INTIMACY

You and your spouse should take this test separately. For each of the statements below, write the number indicating how important that statement is to you in terms of experiencing sexual fulfillment in your marriage, using this scale:

1 – Not that important   **2** – Somewhat important   **3** – Very important

His	Hers	
_____	_____	1. I am the one who is blessed when I provide for my spouse's sexual needs.
_____	_____	2. I find contentment knowing my spouse is contented with our sexual relationship.
_____	_____	3. I know having sex on a regular basis builds a hedge to keep others out.
_____	_____	4. I can't enjoy sex unless I know my spouse has eyes only for me.
_____	_____	5. I find it sexually exciting when my spouse and I look into each other's eyes for a long period of time.
_____	_____	6. I need to be noticed by my spouse during the day to enjoy sex at night.

His   Hers

_____   _____   7. I strongly believe that our sexual intimacy is holy in the sight of God.

_____   _____   8. I find greater sexual fulfillment when we pray before we are intimate.

_____   _____   9. I become sexually excited bringing my spouse to orgasm.

_____   _____   10. I need my spouse to enthusiastically enter into the sexual act with me.

_____   _____   11. I find sexual intimacy meets a deep need in my heart for companionship.

_____   _____   12. I experience sexual attraction for my spouse when we spend the day doing routine tasks together.

_____   _____   13. I am more sexually attracted when my spouse is the spiritual leader in our relationship.

_____   _____   14. I find myself more attracted to my spouse when I watch my spouse pray, study the Bible, and attend church.

_____   _____   15. I need romance with my spouse our entire life for sex to be meaningful.

_____   _____   16. I love it when my spouse stirs my imagination with words.

_____   _____   17. I find security when my spouse takes steps to avoid sexual temptation.

_____   _____   18. I want my spouse to be the one who changes the channel when suggestive images come on the television.

_____   _____   19. I often feel emotionally intoxicated from the pleasures that sexual intercourse provides.

_____   _____   20. I want my spouse to ask me for sex as much as I ask for it.

His   Hers

_____ _____   21. I want my spouse to be my buddy as well as my lover.

_____ _____   22. I feel far less lonely in life when my spouse willingly gives me sex.

_____ _____   23. I want my spouse to find happiness in offering me sex.

_____ _____   24. I experience a special arousal when my spouse is joyful before intimacy.

_____ _____   25. I feel respected when my spouse enjoys the sexual act as much as I do.

_____ _____   26. I want my spouse to feel sex is more a thrill than an obligation.

_____ _____   27. I believe having regular sexual intimacy guards the door of our marriage.

_____ _____   28. I love it when my spouse tells others our love story.

_____ _____   29. I find it is easier for me to experience orgasm when I first lovingly surrender myself to my spouse.

_____ _____   30. I believe it damages a marriage when my spouse withholds sex to gain something.

_____ _____   31. I need my spouse to whisper just the right words to take me to a higher level of arousal.

_____ _____   32. I experience climax sooner when my spouse talks to me during sex.

_____ _____   33. I appreciate it when my spouse makes certain I achieve orgasm first.

_____ _____   34. I feel more loved and respected when my spouse says yes to my request for intimacy.

_____ _____   35. I know having sex with my spouse makes us closer friends.

His   Hers

His   Hers

_____ _____   36. I experience far less isolation in life when our sexual relationship is strong.

_____ _____   37. I feel rejected when my spouse is just waiting for the sexual act to be over.

_____ _____   38. I believe God designed orgasm primarily as a gift of pleasure.

_____ _____   39. I am fulfilled when my spouse consider sex a privilege not a duty.

_____ _____   40. I think it's wrong to withhold sex simply because we've had a disagreement that isn't fully resolved.

_____ _____   41. I find time with just the two of us talking and listening makes me more eager for sex.

_____ _____   42. I love it when time loses its meaning during sex.

_____ _____   43. I like sex because my spouse is my best friend.

_____ _____   44. I feel emotionally bonded to my spouse when they come along with me for everyday chores and responsibilities.

_____ _____   45. I believe watching pornography conveys sends the painful message that I'm not good enough for my spouse.

_____ _____   46. I believe remaining faithful has a huge impact on our children's future.

_____ _____   47. I find deeper sexual satisfaction knowing our sexual relationship pleases God.

_____ _____   48. I know when my spouse makes loving sacrifices for me during the day I'm more eager for sex at night.

_____ _____   49. I feel emotionally bonded to my spouse when they sit and watch a game or movie with me.

_____ _____   50. I would be lost for meaningful relationships if my spouse were to die.

His   Hers

_____   _____   51. I believe emotional camaraderie strengthens our sexual bond.

_____   _____   52. I am turned on when I see my spouse is turned on by the sexual experience.

_____   _____   53. I strongly believe a couple should abstain from sex only if they both agree to it.

_____   _____   54. I want my spouse to understand saying yes to sex often and willingly says I love you.

_____   _____   55. I have found the closer my spouse's walk with God is, the more I enjoy sex.

_____   _____   56. I want my spouse to take the spiritual initiative in our marriage just as much as they take the sexual initiative.

_____   _____   57. I find my deep sexual satisfaction is in knowing I'm my spouse's one and only.

_____   _____   58. I want to remain faithful to my spouse so it will be easier for my children to believe in God.

_____   _____   59. I believe keeping romance alive is vital to keeping sexual intimacy alive.

_____   _____   60. I need my spouse to be as interested in romance as they were when we first met in order to experience sexual fulfillment.

The Romantic Heart gives and receives love by bonding with our eyes, stirring our spouse's emotional imagination with our words and creating intimacy with our time alone together. The following questions pertain to the Romantic Heart. Put the number you scored for each question in the space provided.

His	Hers
5. _____	5. _____
6. _____	6. _____
15. _____	15. _____
16. _____	16. _____
31. _____	31. _____
32. _____	32. _____
41. _____	41. _____
42. _____	42. _____
59. _____	59. _____
60. _____	60. _____

Total Score _____   _____

The Worshiping Heart gives and receives love by exalting in God's presence in sexual intimacy as a couple gives one another sacrificial love and extraordinary honor. The following questions pertain to The Worshiping Heart. Put the number you scored for each question in the blank.

	His	Hers
7.	_____	7. _____
8.	_____	8. _____
13.	_____	13. _____
14.	_____	14. _____
33.	_____	33. _____
34.	_____	34. _____
47.	_____	47. _____
48.	_____	48. _____
55.	_____	55. _____
56.	_____	56. _____
Total Score	_____	_____

The Companion Heart gives and receives love through deep soul-ties, emotional camaraderie, and undying loyalty. It ignites married sexual love because a strong friendship makes for good sex. The following questions pertain to The Companion Heart. Put the number you scored for each question in the blank.

His	Hers
11. _____	11. _____
12. _____	12. _____
21. _____	21. _____
22. _____	22. _____
35. _____	35. _____
36. _____	36. _____
43. _____	43. _____
44. _____	44. _____
49. _____	49. _____
50. _____	50. _____

Total Score _____   _____

The Giving Heart gives and receives love by joyfully providing for the spouse's sexual needs and offering itself in loving surrender. The following questions pertain to the Giving Heart. Put the number you scored for that question in the space provided.

	His		Hers
	1. _____		1. _____
	2. _____		2. _____
	23. _____		23. _____
	24. _____		24. _____
	29. _____		29. _____
	30. _____		30. _____
	39. _____		39. _____
	40. _____		40. _____
	53. _____		53. _____
	54. _____		54. _____
Total Score	_____		_____

The Ecstatic Heart gives and receives love by reveling in the exquisite joy and ecstasy of sharing the sexual act with their life-long spouse. The following questions pertain to The Ecstatic Heart. Put the number you scored for each question in the blank.

	His		Hers
9.	_____	9.	_____
10.	_____	10.	_____
19.	_____	19.	_____
20.	_____	20.	_____
25.	_____	25.	_____
26.	_____	26.	_____
37.	_____	37.	_____
38.	_____	38.	_____
51.	_____	51.	_____
52.	_____	52.	_____
Total Score	_____		_____

The Guardian Heart gives and receives love by keeping the vows of faithfulness, protecting their oneness of flesh and spirits, and drawing future generations to God as a result of relational integrity. The following questions pertain to The Guardian Heart. Put the number you scored for each question in each blank.

	His	Hers
3.	_____	_____
4.	_____	_____
17.	_____	_____
18.	_____	_____
27.	_____	_____
28.	_____	_____
45.	_____	_____
46.	_____	_____
57.	_____	_____
58.	_____	_____
Total Score	_____	_____

Scoring Key:

Add up all of the numbers you marked in each category. The total score in each category is an indication of how important that Heart of Intimacy is to you in experiencing sexual fulfillment with your spouse.

+ A score of 10 indicates it's not very important to you.

+ A score of 11 to 19 indicates it is somewhat important to you.

+ A score of 20 to 30 indicates it is very important to you.

Your top three scores are the three Hearts of Intimacy that are most important to you.

My Top Three Hearts of Intimacy are:

1. _____

2. _____

3. _____

My Spouse's Top Three Hearts of Intimacy are:

1. _____

2. _____

3. _____

Our hope is that you can use this exercise to better understand your spouse and what you can do to strengthen your bonds of marital intimacy.

ABOUT THE AUTHORS

Bob and Cheryl are the co-founders of For Better For Worse For Keeps Ministries, dedicated to healing hearts and restoring marriages in underserved communities. Over the last twenty-five years, they have authored numerous books together on marriage, including *For Better For Worse For Keeps* and *To Have and To Hold*, both of which were nominated for the Gold Medallion Award. Among other titles, they wrote *Marriage Minutes, One Minute Devotionals for Couples, How to Get Your Husband to Talk to You,* and *Marriage Miracle.*

For over a decade, Bob has been the host of a weekly television call-in show, *Marriage – For Better For Worse,* on the Total Living Network. It won "The Best Teaching Television Program of the Year" award given by the National Religious Broadcasters in 2013. In addition, Bob has produced a daily, one-minute program to encourage marriages, *The Marriage Minute.* The program began in 1994 and continues to play on radio stations throughout the United States.

Cheryl, a homemaker and seasoned mother, has served as an author, literary agent, publicist, and writing conference speaker. Together, she and Bob served in the local church for twenty-five years before founding For Better For Worse For Keeps Ministries in 2009.

Bob and Cheryl have been married 39 years and are the parents of six grown children and six grandchildren. For the last three decades, they have made their home in the greater Chicago area. Their best times are with their kids and grandkids as they appreciate their good humor. They love to hike in the woods, fish, travel, and dog-sit for vacationing friends.

They travel throughout the United States speaking and presenting weekend marriage conferences and marriage ministry training seminars. If you wish to contact them for a speaking engagement or marriage conference, visit their website: www.forkeepsministries.com.